A Family Journey with Jesus through Lent

Prayers & Activities for Each Day

P9-EKS-035

A Family Journey with Jesus through Lent

Prayers & Activities for Each Day

Angela M. Burrin

The Word Among Us
9639 Doctor Perry Road
Ijamsville, Maryland 21754
www.wordamongus.org
ISBN: 978-1-59325-050-8

Copyright © 2004 by The Word Among Us Press
All rights reserved.

Cover and book design: David Crosson
Cover and inside illustrations by Jim Higgins

14 13 12 11 10   4 5 6 7 8

Scripture passages contained herein are from the New Revised Standard Version Bible: Catholic Edition, copyright © 1989, 1993, by the Division of Christian Education of the National Council of the Churches of Christ in the United States of America. Used by permission. All rights reserved.

No part of this publication may be reproduced, stored in a retrieval system, or transmitted in any form or by any means—electronic, mechanical, photocopy, recording, or any other—except for brief quotations in printed reviews, without the prior permission of the publisher.

Made and printed in the United States of America

Theological Advisor: Fr. Joseph Wimmer, OSA

Library of Congress Control Number: 2004115421

Table of Contents

Acknowledgments

To Patricia Mitchell, for sharing with me the excitement of writing this book.
We had a lot of fun! I'm so grateful for the support of her creative input and editing skills.
Thanks, Patty.

To Margaret Procario, for an excellent job in putting the finishing touches to the text.

To Jim Higgins, for adding greatly to the book by taking my words and transforming them into sketches.

To David Crosson, whose artistic talent has pulled all the elements together and made this book such a delight.

To Fr. Joe Wimmer, for his thorough theological review.

Most importantly, thank you, Jesus, for everything!

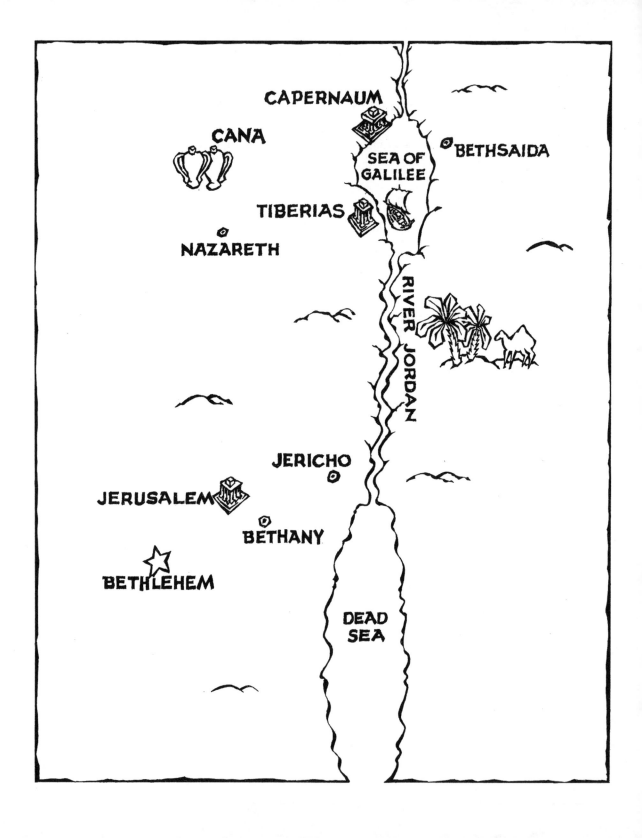

Introduction

You and your family are about to embark on a journey back in time to first-century Palestine. There you will meet Hebrew children from places like Capernaum, Nazareth, Bethany, and Cana. You will learn about the lives of Sarah, Benjamin, Samuel, and others—what they eat, how they worship, and what kind of work their parents do. Most important, you will learn about Jesus, whose amazing miracles and challenging teachings caused so much excitement and debate in their cities, towns, and neighborhoods.

A Family Journey with Jesus through Lent features a story for each of the forty days of Lent, beginning on Ash Wednesday with Jesus' baptism in the River Jordan and ending with his resurrection on Easter Sunday. After each story, Jesus speaks lovingly and personally to the children about the significance of the parable, miracle, or event that was told. Each day ends with a Scripture verse the family can memorize together, along with a short closing prayer.

This book was conceived and written as a way to promote family prayer. So many parents desire to pray together as a family but are at a loss for what to do that will keep their children interested and positive about the experience. *A Family Journey with Jesus through Lent* answers that need by providing a format for prayer and reflection on Scripture. It is our hope that, as the children become engaged in the characters and stories, they will eagerly look forward to the next story—and the next day of prayer. Although this book was written specifically for Lent, it can be used at other times of the year to enliven Scripture and bring about a deeper understanding of the Catholic faith.

Why is it important to pray as a family? As the Second Vatican Council taught, our families are the "domestic church." Parents are the "first herald of the gospel for their children," according to Pope John Paul II. By praying with their children, reading Scripture to them, and introducing them to the sacraments and the Church, parents become "fully parents"—they have not only transmitted bodily life but also the life of the Spirit through the cross and resurrection of Jesus (*Familiaris Consortio*, 39).

Parents can encourage children from a very young age to make Jesus their Lord, their Savior, and their friend. In my own years as a teacher and an elementary school principal, I witnessed the enthusiasm of children who read, heard, and acted out gospel stories. Through those stories, the children came to see Jesus as a very real person, who not only lived in a specific time and place in history but still lives among us today. As their knowledge of Jesus grew, their relationship with him deepened, along with their confidence that he loves them unconditionally and wants to be involved in every aspect of their lives.

How to Use This Book

Choose a special time and place where you will meet every day during Lent to read, discuss, and pray about one of the stories in this book. Mornings or evenings are natural times for families to gather together, but any time of the day will work, as long as it is uninterrupted.

Parents can choose to read the stories to their children or can ask those children who are old enough to take turns reading the stories aloud. Children will be excited when a Hebrew child they have already "met" relates another story later in the book. They will enjoy using the map on page 8 to find the cities or towns where the Hebrew children live. And they will have fun searching the drawings in the book to find people and objects described in the narratives.

The section "Jesus, Speak to Me" is written as if Jesus is talking to the children and encourages them to make the leap from the story to a specific theme. Among the themes explored are the importance of generosity, forgiveness, and prayer, and the meaning of the Sacraments of Baptism, Reconciliation, and the Eucharist. Often there is an invitation for parents and children to talk about the issue. Your child may be willing to talk at that moment, or you may want to bring up the subject later, perhaps at dinner. Other actions are sometimes suggested, such as performing a kind act. Be creative and, whenever possible, try to follow through on the suggestions. They will help your children see that their faith can be lived out in concrete ways.

The "Remember" section sums up the major theme of that day's story, which you can reinforce by mentioning it again later in the day or week. You can also reinforce the "Scripture Memory Verse" by asking your child to write it down and post it where everyone will see it, such as on your refrigerator. Creating this "storehouse" of memorized Scripture verses for your children will serve them for the rest of their lives. Perhaps you can play a family quiz game to see who has the best memory! Each day's material ends with a brief prayer, which you might want to recite together again when your child goes to bed.

This book does not include stories for Sundays, since they are not officially counted in the forty days of Lent. This might be a good day for one of the activities we have described on pages 186-190. Activities are included for both Lent and Holy Week. Choose the activities that are the most age-appropriate for your family, and don't feel compelled to do all of them. Perhaps these will become Lenten family traditions for years to come.

As your Lenten journey with Jesus comes to an end, we pray that these Scripture stories will have brought Jesus into your home and life in a new and deeper way. For every member of your family, may your Easter be filled with the joy of the risen Christ!

Angela M. Burrin

A Family Journey with Jesus through Lent
First Week
of Lent

week 1 | day 1

The Baptism of Jesus (Matthew 3:1–17)

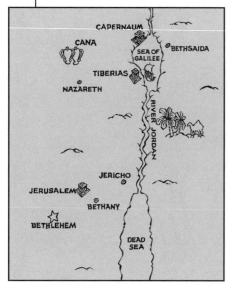

My name is Joshua. I'm twelve. Joseph, my brother, is ten. We live in Bethsaida, which is east of the River Jordan. This river flows down through the middle of my country, Palestine. We also have two big seas—the Sea of Galilee and the Dead Sea. The Sea of Galilee is teeming with fish because it's filled with fresh water. But nothing lives in the Dead Sea because it's so salty!

Let me tell you about my house. It's made of mud and brick, and it has only one room, with small slits for windows. The flat roof is made of wooden beams, covered with straw and clay. My family often sits on the roof in the evenings to talk or play board games. The roof is also a great place to dry our clothes. We lay out grapes, and the sun turns them into raisins. On hot nights I like to sleep up there to feel the cool breeze.

Now it's time to tell you my story about Jesus. The first time I saw him was at the River Jordan. That morning my brother, Joseph, and I were playing with marbles in front of our house. There were so many people passing by our home on the way to the river that I said to Joseph, "Something special must be happening down at the river." Then we heard someone say, "John the Baptist is here!" We ran inside our house to tell our parents. My father said, "This man is a prophet. We must go and see him." So we hurried toward the river with the others.

On the way, Father explained that a prophet is someone who is given a special message by God to tell the people. I wondered what John the Baptist's message would be. When we got to the river, I was surprised to see him standing in the water up to his waist! His camel's-hair tunic and leather belt were hanging on a nearby tree. Father told me that when John the Baptist was living in the desert, he ate locusts and wild honey. I liked the thought of eating honey—but not locusts!

John the Baptist wasn't alone in the river. Other people were there with him. I was really curious. "What's happening? Why is he getting them so wet?" I asked my father. Before he could answer, I heard John the Baptist say, "God wants all of you to be sorry for the things you have done wrong. Let him change your heart. Come and tell God here in the water the ways you have disobeyed his commandments. Receive baptism!" I thought to myself, "That's the message God has given him!"

> **Remember**
>
> Jesus loves me! He's happy that I'm part of his family, and he wants to give me grace to walk with him through Lent.

I watched as men and women, young and old, walked into the river. After they had told God that they were sorry and wanted to live good lives, John baptized them by lowering them into the water. That was a sign that God had forgiven them. Now I knew why John was called "the Baptist."

John spoke to the people again: "I am baptizing you with water, but when the Christ comes, he will baptize you with the Holy Spirit. I'm not good enough to carry even his sandals." "Father," I asked, "when do you think the Christ will come?" Just then Father saw Jesus coming toward us down the hillside. He recognized Jesus because he had grown up with him in Nazareth, in Galilee. "Joshua," said Father, "there's Jesus, the carpenter's son."

> ## Scripture Memory Verse
>
> "This is my Son, the Beloved, with whom I am well pleased."
>
> (Matthew 3:17)

We watched as Jesus walked into the water toward John. It looked like Jesus wanted to be baptized, too! John was very surprised and said, "Jesus, I should be baptized by you." But Jesus replied, "John, it is right for you to baptize me." So John poured water over Jesus.

Then an amazing thing happened. Just as Jesus was walking out of the water, a dove hovered over him, and a voice from heaven said, "This is my Son, whom I love; with him I am well pleased."

"Oh Father," I asked, "is Jesus the Christ? Is he the one that we heard about in the prophecies?" "Yes, Joshua!" Father exclaimed. "I do believe now that Jesus is the Holy One sent by God."

Jesus, Speak to Me

The day that I was baptized by John in the River Jordan was an important one for me. It was wonderful to hear my Father in heaven tell me that he loved me and was pleased with me.

The day you were baptized was a very special day for me, too. That was the day that you became part of God's family. I have always loved you, and I have always wanted you to be one with our heavenly Father and me. Ask your parents about the day you received the Sacrament of Baptism. Perhaps they have photos of you in a special white garment that was a sign of your new life with me.

Did you know that at your baptism you received special graces? Another word for grace is "heavenly help." I'm sure that there are lots of times during your day when you need help.

Prayer

Jesus, thank you for loving me. I'm so grateful that I have been baptized and am now part of God's family.

Perhaps you are going to do something special during Lent, like giving some of your own money to the poor or helping someone in need. Perhaps you are going to give up something you like, such as eating sweets or watching television. Please ask for heavenly help as you journey with me through Lent. Maybe you can start a journal, so that you can write down everything you want to remember about our journey together. I'm looking forward to spending the forty days of Lent with you!

Forty Days in the Desert (Matthew 4:1–11)

Today it's my turn to tell you a story about Jesus. My name is Hannah. I'm eleven years old. My sister, Leah, is nine, and my brother, Daniel, is seven. Last year my grandfather came to live with us here in Tiberias, on the Sea of Galilee. I love listening to his stories!

Grandfather used to travel around selling the olives from his groves. He would take two or three donkeys loaded with baskets of olives from Galilee, in the North, to Judea, in the South. His trips took him over the rocky hillsides and through the lush, green valleys along the River Jordan. Every day he would stop at a different market to sell his olives. At night he would stay at a nearby inn. As he ate dinner he would chat with other merchants, who had come from different parts of the country and sometimes from foreign countries. Grandfather even met people who had traveled across the hot desert sands. I don't think I would want to spend even one day in the desert. Would you?

But Jesus didn't spend just one day in the desert—he spent forty days there. How do I know that? My grandfather told me. You see, my grandfather is a friend of Peter, one of Jesus' disciples!

After Jesus was baptized by John in the River Jordan, the Holy Spirit told him to go into the desert. Jesus crossed the river and walked to the desert west of the Dead Sea, in Judea. It was a very difficult time. Jesus

Remember

Satan has been defeated by Jesus' death on the cross. With Scripture I can fight temptations.

was alone in the middle of miles and miles of sand. The only things he saw were a few bushes here and there, and some birds and wild animals. In the daytime Jesus had to try to find a rock to shade him from the hot sun. At night, when the desert got cold, he shivered, because he didn't have a blanket to keep him warm or a tent to protect him from the wind. And he was hungry, because he didn't have anything to eat or drink for the entire forty days and nights.

Now Satan, who had tempted Adam and Eve in the Garden of Eden, knew that Jesus was probably feeling very weak. So he thought, "I'm going to tempt Jesus to do something wrong." But what Satan didn't know was that Jesus loved his Father so much that he would never disobey him.

This was Satan's first temptation: He said, "Jesus, you must be very hungry. If you are really the Son of God, why don't you turn these stones into bread?" Quoting Scripture, Jesus replied, "I will not listen to you. My heavenly Father will provide all that I need."

Satan tried a second time. He took Jesus to Jerusalem. "Jesus," he said, "if you are really the Son of God, throw yourself down from the highest point of the

Temple. I know the angels will take care of you." Jesus answered again with Scripture. "Satan, I will not do that. I will not put my Father to the test."

Satan had one last temptation. He took Jesus to a very high sand dune and said, "Everything you see down there, Jesus, is mine. If you bow down and worship me, I will give it all to you." Once again Jesus quoted from Scripture. "Away with you, Satan. I will worship only my Father in heaven. I want to serve him alone."

> **Scripture Memory Verse**
>
> "Blessed is anyone who endures temptation."
>
> (James 1:12)

After those three temptations, Satan knew that he just couldn't tempt Jesus to do anything wrong. So he left.

Now Jesus' Father in heaven had seen everything that was happening to him. For forty days and nights he had watched Jesus. He knew that he was hungry and thirsty. He knew how hard Satan had tried to tempt him. God was very pleased with his Son! In fact, he was so pleased that he sent angels from heaven to take care of all his needs.

It was after that very hard time in the desert that Jesus met my grandfather's friend and started his public ministry.

Jesus, Speak to Me

As you can imagine, I was very hungry, thirsty, and tired during those forty days in the desert. But all the time, I was thinking about how much my Father loved me. That helped me, especially when Satan tempted me.

Satan is always looking for people to tempt. He doesn't want God to be loved. He doesn't love God, and he doesn't want to be obedient to God. He doesn't want people to show their love for their Father in heaven by doing what they know is right.

Please remember that I know what it is like to be tempted to do something wrong. There are times when you too will be tempted—perhaps to cheat, to lie, or to disobey your parents. Right then and there, you have a choice to make. You can say no to Satan!

How do you say no to Satan? Sometimes you need to walk away from the temptation. Sometimes you can quote a Scripture passage that you have memorized, like I did. Sometimes you need to tell your mother or father about the temptation so that they can help you. Above all, remember to ask me to help you. It makes me so happy when you fight temptation so that you can live a good life.

The Calling of the First Disciples

(Matthew 4:18–22; Luke 5:1–11)

I'm Jacob, and I'm eight years old. I have a twin sister named Sarah. My brother, David, is ten, and my sister Rebekah is twelve. We live in a city called Capernaum, on the Sea of Galilee. Jesus spent a lot of time with the people around the shores of the lake—that's what we call the Sea of Galilee.

Guess what my father does for a living? He's a fisherman. Every day David and I go down to the lake to help Father mend his nets. Sometimes we even go out fishing with him. I'm learning how to clean the fish that we catch. That's not my favorite job! But Father says that I need to know how to do it if I want to become a fisherman like him.

One day, David and I were mending some fishing nets with our father when we saw a crowd of people gathering. "Come, boys," said Father, "let's go see what's happening." No sooner had we left our nets than we met one of my friends, who said, "Jacob, guess what? Jesus is here!" Everyone was really excited to see Jesus, because we had heard about his baptism by John in the River Jordan. Although we didn't know much about Jesus, we did know that he was a very special man.

Father really wanted to hear what Jesus was saying to the crowd, so we got as close as we could. For a little while, Jesus walked along the edge of the water. Then he stopped, turned toward the crowd, and said, "My heavenly Father loves all of you so much. Be sorry and repent of all that you have done wrong. Believe the good news that my heavenly Father wants to forgive your sins." Just then Jesus looked at me. His eyes were so kind that I said to myself, "Jesus really loves me."

> **Remember**
> Jesus wants to have a personal relationship with you, just as he did with his disciples.

But that's not the end of my story. Until this time, Jesus was alone. He wanted to have some men to help him tell everyone the good news of his Father's love. This turned out to be a really exciting day for some of the fishermen in my town.

Jesus continued walking. Then, looking straight at two fishermen, Jesus stopped and said, "Follow me, and I will make you fishers of men." The fishermen were two of my father's friends, Simon Peter and his brother, Andrew. Immediately, they dropped their nets and followed Jesus. They must have felt very special to know that Jesus wanted them to join him.

Jesus walked a little farther and then stopped again. He called out to two more fishermen—James and his brother, John—who were in their boat getting their nets ready to fish. "Will you two follow me?" Jesus asked. "Yes, Jesus, we will," they answered. Then they jumped out of their boat, turned and said good-bye to their father, and followed Jesus. They left their father, Zebedee, sitting alone in the boat. Zebedee must have been very surprised that James and John were following Jesus.

Scripture Memory Verse

"Follow me, and I will make you fishers of men."

(Matthew 4:19)

Then I heard Jesus say to Simon Peter, "Row out into the deep water and let down your nets for a catch." Simon Peter replied, "But Jesus, we have been fishing all night and haven't caught a thing. But because you say so, I will let down the nets." Do you want to know what happened? Immediately a great school of fish swam right into the nets. From the beach, I watched the fishermen struggle to pull in the nets. I heard them call for help to their friends in another boat. That boat pulled up next to theirs, and together all the men managed to pull the nets in before they broke. There were so many fish that both boats nearly sank!

Jesus, Speak to Me

I was very happy the day that Andrew, Simon Peter, James, and John accepted my invitation to come and be my disciples. I was so pleased that their hearts were open to saying yes. In the next few weeks I asked others to join me. Now I was no longer alone but had friends to help me spread the good news of God's love.

Today I have an invitation for you. I'm inviting you to be one of my special friends—to have a personal relationship with me and to be my follower! I promise I will always be a good friend to you and never leave you. I love listening to you. Talk to me about your days. Tell me the things that are important to you. You can tell me anything! Ask me to help you make good choices. Invite me to be a part of everything you do.

Prayer

Thank you, Jesus, for inviting me to be one of your special friends. Jesus, I love you. Please come into my life, and help me to tell all my friends about your love.

The Wedding Feast at Cana

(John 2:1–12)

Welcome to Cana! My name is Esther, and I'm ten. When I was born, my mother called me her "little queen" because she was so happy to have a baby girl—she already had four sons. So she named me after Queen Esther.

I like to help my mom take care of our home. Two of my jobs are sweeping the earthen floor and going to the well to get drinking water. Each day Mother makes bread—lots of it, because we eat it at every meal! She mixes barley flour with water and salt, and then she kneads the dough. Sometimes she adds yeast, which makes the bread rise. But usually we have flat bread. After she has pressed the dough into a round circle, she bakes it in a stone oven.

Everyone in Cana knows that Mother is a great cook. So when my aunt needed someone to help prepare the food for her daughter's wedding, she asked my mom if she would do it. Of course Mother was thrilled to be asked. She turned to me and said, "Esther, it's going to be a lot of hard work, but together we can do it." We heard that Jesus was going to be a guest at the wedding. We were so excited!

> **Remember**
>
> I'm going to listen for Jesus' voice. He loves to speak to me!

Jewish weddings here usually last about a week. They are so much fun! There is plenty of eating, drinking, singing, and dancing. New guests come and go all week. So Mother knew she had to make a lot of special party food! After a week of cooking, Mother had baskets of special breads and cheeses, pots of lamb, chicken, and lentil stews, and bowls of olives, grapes, figs, dates, and pomegranates. "Esther, we did it!" Mother said.

After the wedding ceremony at the local synagogue, the party began. I saw Jesus among the guests along with Mary, his mother, and some of his disciples. Everyone was having a great time celebrating with the bride and bridegroom. And everyone loved Mother's food!

Then I noticed Jesus' mother looking very worried. "What's wrong?" I thought. I heard Mary say to Jesus, "They have no more wine." Jesus quietly replied, "Mother, my special time for miracles hasn't come yet." But Mary knew Jesus' heart and said to the servants, "Do whatever he tells you."

I kept watching Jesus, wondering if he would do anything. He did! He instructed the servants to fill six stone jars with water. They filled them to the brim with water from the well. The jars were so large that it took two men to

Scripture Memory Verse

"Do whatever he tells you."

(John 2:5)

lift each one. But with many servants helping, it didn't take too long.

Then Jesus said, "Pour some out and give it to the head server." The head server tasted it. You should have seen the look of surprise on his face. "This is great wine!" I heard him say to the bridegroom. "Why have you saved the best for last? We usually serve the best wine first, and then when everyone has had too much to drink, we serve the cheaper wine. But you have saved the best until now."

That was Jesus' very first miracle. I was there, and I saw it!

Jesus, Speak to Me

When I changed water into wine, my Father's power was working through me. That helped my disciples, and others, to believe that I am the Son of God and the Savior of the world.

Do you remember the words that my mother, Mary, said to the servants? "Do whatever he tells you." Well, those are the same words Mary is saying to you today. Yes, more than two thousand years later, I still have something to tell you. Are you wondering how you will know what I am saying to you? If you listen very carefully, I will speak to you through my Holy Spirit. I might speak to you when you go to Mass, when you read the Bible in your prayer time, or through your parents, your teachers, and other adults.

Listen for my Holy Spirit throughout your day. Perhaps I want you to call your friend who is ill, or to do something kind for your mother or father. Be open to what I ask you to do each day. What great things you will do to build my kingdom on earth when you listen to me!

Prayer

Jesus, I'm so pleased that you want to speak to me. Help me to be a good listener.

A Family Journey with Jesus through Lent
Second Week of Lent

The Healing of the Blind Man Bartimaeus

(Mark 10:46–52; Luke 18:35–43)

My name is Samuel, and I'm from Jericho. I'll be ten next week. I'm proud to live in this famous city. Do you remember the story of Joshua and the Battle of Jericho? It's true that the walls came tumbling down! Well, I want to tell you two stories—one today and one tomorrow—about what happened when Jesus came to Jericho.

It was Sunday, the day after the Sabbath and the first day of the week. The Sabbath is our day of rest. No one is allowed to work from sunset on Friday to sunset on Saturday. On the Sabbath, we go to the synagogue, which is the building where we worship God. When the men pray, they wear blue-striped shawls with knotted tassels to remind them of God's laws.

That Sunday, I woke up just before dawn, as soon as our neighbor's cock started crowing. That's my signal every morning to get up. It's not always easy—sometimes I want to turn over and go back to sleep! But I'd had a good night's rest, and I was ready to start the first day of the week. For me that meant going up on the roof to get some dried straw and branches so that my mother could light the oven.

As I was standing there looking out over the rooftops, I saw about twenty of our neighbors heading toward the gates of the city. I wondered what was happening. Then someone called out, "Jesus is coming to Jericho today, and we want to see if he will perform any miracles." I knew that Jesus had made sick people better. I was so excited that he was coming to Jericho. I quickly gathered up the straw and branches and ran down the steps from the roof. Before even reaching the doorway, I shouted, "Mother, Jesus is coming to town. Can I go and see him?" She said, "Let's skip breakfast and all go."

> **Remember**
>
> Jesus wants to open my eyes so that I can appreciate all his gifts to me.

We ran along some of the narrow streets and out through one of the gates. Now that we were outside the city walls, we saw Jesus in the distance, coming toward us with some of his disciples. Jericho is a busy city, and people with disabilities often sit by the gates begging for money so that they can buy food for themselves and their families. On this day there was a blind man begging by the gates. I felt so sorry for him as he sat there, waiting for people to put money into his bowl. My mother handed me a few coins to give him, and he thanked me. When I asked him his name, he said, "Bartimaeus."

The crowd was really noisy, and there was a lot of commotion. "He's nearly here!" one of the men announced. Bartimaeus asked, "What's happening?" "Jesus of Nazareth is passing by," another man told him. Then Bartimaeus called out, "Jesus, Son of David, have mercy on me." "Quiet down!" someone in the crowd said to him, but Bartimaeus yelled even louder, "Son of David, have mercy on me!" Bartimaeus really wanted Jesus to heal his eyes so he could see.

Scripture Memory Verse

"Lord, let me see again."

(Luke 18:41)

But Jesus had heard Bartimaeus' cry. He stopped and asked for the man to be brought to him. Jesus asked, "What do you want me to do for you?" "Lord, I want to see," the blind man replied. Jesus said, "Bartimaeus, receive your sight. Your faith has saved you." Immediately, Bartimaeus could see! Praising God, he jumped up and followed Jesus into the city. All of us in the crowd joined in singing, dancing, and praising God for this wonderful miracle. What a great morning—and all before breakfast!

Jesus, Speak to Me

Bartimaeus knew that I could help him to see. His faith really pleased me. I would like you to have faith in me so that I can give you "spiritual" sight. With this kind of sight, you will recognize all the wonderful gifts I have given you. It's so easy to take things for granted, isn't it?

I want to open your eyes to see the beauty of my creation. I want to open your eyes to see how much your parents love you and how often they serve you. I want you to see that I provide for all that you need. With your new spiritual sight, you will become so much more appreciative of all that you have and all that I have done for you.

This week during Lent, why don't you write down the things you don't want to take for granted any longer. Keep a list in your journal. Every so often, read your list and add to it. Maybe you could write a prayer of thanksgiving for everything you can see with your new spiritual sight.

Prayer

Jesus, I want you to open my eyes to really see all that is around me.

Zaccaeus, the Tax Collector

(Luke 19:1–10)

Hello again! Remember me? I'm Samuel, who told you the story yesterday of how Jesus healed the blind man, Bartimaeus. Now I want to tell you my second story.

After we saw Jesus heal Bartimaeus, we went home to have breakfast. As we ate our barley bread, goat cheese, and olives, we talked excitedly about the miraculous healing. Then I went outside to play marbles with my friend Jethro. I just happened to look up for a moment, and I saw Jesus walking right past us. I was so surprised! I picked up my marbles and rushed into the house to ask my mother if I could follow Jesus. "Go ahead, Samuel. Perhaps Jesus will heal someone else today." "Thanks, Mom," I shouted as I ran after Jesus.

There is one thing I need to tell you about where we live. The Romans have ruled over us for a long time. They order every family here in Palestine to give them money. We call this paying taxes to Caesar, the ruler in Rome. Some of our own people work for the Romans by collecting the taxes. In Jericho, there's a man called Zacchaeus, who is in charge of all of them. He's very rich. Tax collectors are not always honest. They often collect extra money from people and then keep some for themselves. As you can imagine, tax collectors are not very popular around here!

But on this afternoon I wasn't thinking about tax collectors. I just wanted to follow Jesus! I loved being near him. I could hear everything he said. Jesus had a kind word for everyone. And I wasn't the only one following him. There were lots and lots of people. Finally he stopped and began talking to a whole group of people. By now I was tired, so I ran ahead and climbed a sycamore tree. That way I could rest and still see Jesus and hear what he had to say.

> **Remember**
>
> Jesus wants me to make things right when I have done wrong, just like Zacchaeus did.

Just as I settled down on one of the higher branches, I saw a really short man climb the sycamore tree next to mine. I recognized him—he was Zacchaeus, the tax collector! He must have wanted to see Jesus, too. But he was so short that he couldn't see Jesus above the crowd. He had the same idea I did of climbing a tree!

Jesus taught the people for a little while. Then he passed by me and stopped. He looked up at the tree next to mine—the one where the chief tax collector was sitting—and said, "Zacchaeus, hurry and come down; for I must stay at your house today." You should have seen how quickly Zacchaeus got down from that sycamore tree! I heard him say, "Jesus, you are very welcome to come to my home." Some of the people standing around were really surprised and said, "How terrible. Jesus wants to go to the house of a tax collector. Zacchaeus isn't a good man—he's a sinner."

But it didn't matter what people said. That afternoon a very special change came about in Zacchaeus' heart. He said, "Look, Jesus. Here and now I will give half of my possessions to the poor, and if I have cheated anybody out of any money, I will pay them back four times the amount." Jesus smiled and said, "Zacchaeus, I am so happy that you are sorry today for all the wrong things you have done. That is why I am going from village to village, telling everyone to repent of their sins. For the Son of Man came to seek out and to save the lost."

Scripture Memory Verse

"The Son of Man came to seek out and to save the lost."

(Luke 19:10)

Zacchaeus received a very special kind of healing that day. He was healed from a hard heart. I'm so happy that I was there to see it!

Jesus, Speak to Me

Zacchaeus looked into his heart and knew that he needed to change some of the things he was doing. Zacchaeus made things right with the people he had cheated. He gave them even more money than he had taken from them, and he said, "I am very sorry for what I did to you." There was great rejoicing in heaven that day when Zacchaeus, a sinner, repented!

Each day I want you to do what Zacchaeus did. I want you to look into your heart and see if you need to say you are sorry. The Holy Spirit will show you where you need to change. Perhaps you can look over your day before you go to bed, as part of your nighttime prayers.

If the Holy Spirit shows you that you have hurt someone, try to make things right with that person as soon as possible. I will give you the courage to do this. And remember, whenever you ask me for forgiveness for something you've done wrong, I will always forgive you.

Prayer

Jesus, thank you for your forgiving heart.

The Parable of the Lost Sheep

(Luke 15:4–7; John 10:1–17)

I'm David, the brother of Rebekah, Jacob, and Sarah. I was named after King David. My parents love reading the Scriptures. Sometimes we read about David, the shepherd boy who killed the Philistine giant, Goliath. David became the king of Israel. We often sing the psalms he wrote.

My favorite psalm is the one about the Lord as our shepherd. That's probably because my uncle is a shepherd, and I spend a lot of time up in the hills with him. We are out in all kinds of weather, leading the sheep and goats to good grass and water. Mother made me a cloak of sheepskin to keep me warm. My uncle and I always carry a crook. That's a long stick with a hook on the end for pulling out sheep that get trapped in bushes or stuck between rocks. We also carry two weapons to protect the sheep from wild dogs and wolves. One is a sling for hurling stones, and the other is a wooden rod that has pieces of flint tied to it.

Early one morning, as I was walking into the hills to help my uncle tend the sheep, Jesus came again to Capernaum. As soon as people knew that he was back, they started to gather around him. I asked my uncle if I could go see Jesus, too. People with a lot of different jobs left what they were doing and came to hear what Jesus had to say. In the crowd there were even some tax collectors and other people who were known as "sinners" because they weren't living good lives.

When Jesus taught people about the kingdom of God, he often told stories called parables, using everyday things like coins, vineyards, farmers, seeds, or oil lamps to make a point. He must have been looking out toward the sheep on the hillside that morning when he told us this parable:

> **Remember**
>
> Jesus is my Good Shepherd, who knows everything about me! Jesus wants me to stay close to him so that I won't stray from him like the lost sheep.

"Imagine you are a shepherd, and you own a hundred sheep. You are very proud to have so many. Every day you move the sheep from one place to another so that they will always have plenty of grass to graze on. You do this by whistling and calling out to them. The sheep know your whistle and your voice, and they obey you. You love being up on the hillside because it is so peaceful, except when the wolves come to attack your sheep. Then you have to yell and make a lot of noise and throw stones to frighten them away. Sometimes you stay up all night to protect your sheep.

"Because you love your sheep, you count them every day to make sure that you haven't lost any. Then one day you count only ninety-nine sheep. What are you going to do? Are you going to say, 'Oh, I've still got ninety-nine sheep. It doesn't matter that I've lost one'? Or will you say, 'I must go out and find the one sheep that has wandered away and can't hear my whistle'? So off you go, looking for that lost sheep. You hope that a wild animal hasn't eaten it.

Suddenly you hear a faint bleating. You know that it's your lost sheep. You follow the sound. 'There's my lost sheep!' you cry out. 'Oh no, it's caught in a thorn bush!' So you get your crook and carefully lift it out. You put it on your shoulders. Then you walk back to the rest of the flock and gently put it down. You are so happy to have found the sheep that was lost!"

Scripture Memory Verse

"I am the Good Shepherd. I know my own and my own know me."

(John 10:14)

Many people thought Jesus' parable was over, but he said, "Wait! There's more I want to tell you. I want you to know that there is more rejoicing in heaven when one person says, 'I am so sorry, God, for the things I have done wrong,' than there is over ninety-nine other people who are already living good lives." I really think that the tax collectors and others like them in the crowd were rejoicing when they heard Jesus' parable. Perhaps that day many told God they were sorry.

After hearing that parable, I thought to myself, "Jesus would make a wonderful shepherd. He is so caring." It was then that Jesus said, "I am the Good Shepherd. I know my sheep and my sheep know me." Just think! Jesus is my Shepherd, and I am one of his sheep. Jesus knows me!

Jesus, Speak to Me

Yes, I am your Good Shepherd! My heavenly Father loved you so much that he sent me from heaven to earth to lead you on your journey to heaven. Close your eyes and imagine that you are talking to me. What are we saying to each other?

I want you to know how very much I love you. I know where you are and what you are doing every minute of the day. There is nothing you will ever do that could possibly stop me from loving you!

A shepherd makes sure that his sheep are safe and protected. As your Good Shepherd, I want to help you stay close to me so that you will be safe. I want to protect you from places and people that will take you away from me. One way to stay close to me is to pray during the day. Whenever you think of me, ask me to help you deal with the challenges you face. Thank me for the things I have done for you. And tell me how much you love me. Perhaps you could keep a small cross or rosary in your pocket to remind you that I am always with you.

Maybe you and your parents could take a few minutes now to think of ways to stay close to me each day. How can you make sure you don't stray from me? How can you make sure you stay away from people and places that could hurt you?

Prayer

Father, thank you for Jesus, my Good Shepherd. Holy Spirit, please help me to stay close to Jesus.

Jesus Blesses the Children

(Luke 18:15–17; Matthew 19:1–5)

Welcome back to Bethsaida. I am Joseph, Joshua's brother. Unlike the Joseph that I read about in the Torah, who was thrown into a pit by his eleven brothers, I have one brother who is very kind to me! My father is hoping that I will follow in his footsteps and become a carpenter—just like Joseph, the foster father of Jesus.

Which brings me to my story about Jesus. It was a warm summer morning, and Father and I were finishing a table that he was making for a neighbor. I have learned so much about carpentry working with my father. I've even gone with him when he's been asked to help build houses. He has taught me how to use all of his tools. It's fun banging in nails with the mallet. I've only hit my thumb three times! Just recently, Father showed me how to plane wood to make it smooth. I was concentrating really hard on smoothing out the top of the table when my mother came up from the village well. Excitedly she told my father that Jesus was expected to arrive that afternoon. With a big smile on his face, Father said, "Mother, would you like us all to go and see Jesus?"

Joshua was the first to spot the big crowd on the hillside. "Look, everyone, over there! That must be where Jesus is." We headed toward the hillside. We weren't the only families looking for Jesus. Everyone wanted to see him. Mothers were carrying babies. Fathers had toddlers on their shoulders. Wherever I looked, I saw children running toward Jesus. There was so much excitement in the air!

> ## Remember
> Jesus is never too busy to listen to children. I can always go to him in prayer, and he will listen to me.

Jesus was sitting on a large stone, speaking to the Pharisees, when we got to him. While Jesus was speaking, some of the moms and dads started bringing their children right up to him for a blessing. But Jesus' disciples stopped them. "Get back," they said. "Jesus is busy talking. Don't interrupt him. Take your children away." Some of the mothers had tears in their eyes.

But Jesus called the parents back to him. "I love the children. Let them come to me. The kingdom of God belongs to them," he said. I rushed forward and sat down right at Jesus' feet. Jesus patted me on my head. Anna, a girl from my neighborhood, gave Jesus some flowers that she had picked especially for him. He gave her the most wonderful smile. My friends Jesse and Boaz gave him some grapes and a handful of olives. He said, "Thank you. I'll eat these later." It was so much fun talking with Jesus. Then Jesus said, "I want you to know that I love each one of you very much. Never forget that. Will you all please choose every day to be obedient to your parents and to love your brothers and sisters?" I looked into his kind eyes and said, "I will, Jesus."

Scripture Memory Verse

"Let the little children come to me."

(Luke 18:16)

That afternoon all the children were given a big hug by Jesus and a special blessing. You should have seen the happy smiles on the faces of our mothers and fathers! Looking up, Jesus told the crowd: "Truly, whoever does not receive the kingdom of God like a little child will never enter it."

Jesus, Speak to Me

I had such a good time with the children that day. My disciples were worried that I would be annoyed with the children, but of course I wasn't. I love children. All of you who are listening to these stories are important to me. Whenever you talk to me, I listen. I listen to all your prayers.

I want all children to be important to you, too. Will you always take care of each other? Please watch out for those children who don't have any friends. Perhaps they would like to be *your* friend.

During Lent, pray for children all over the world. Pray especially for those who are in the hospital or have physical or mental disabilities, and for

Prayer

Jesus, even though I am a child, I am important to you. Thank you for your love and concern.

those whose parents have died in wars or from diseases or famine. Pray also for the children who are not yet born, that their lives will be protected and that they will have a safe birth.

week 2 | day 5

Jesus Calms the Storm

(Mark 4:35–41)

Do you like storms? I don't mind them if I'm safe inside my house. But they are very frightening if you are outside, and the thunder is loud, the lightning is streaking across the sky, and the winds are making the trees bend over. I want to tell you what happened to Philip—he's my father's friend and one of Jesus' disciples—when he was on the lake in Peter's boat during a storm.

But before I begin, let me introduce myself. I'm Jacob's twin sister, Sarah. So you are back again in the city of Capernaum at the top of the Sea of Galilee. It's very beautiful here. At some places the lake is so wide that you can't even see land on the other side. The lake can also be a dangerous place for fishermen, especially if their boats are a long way off from the shore in deep water. That's because fierce winds and violent storms often happen suddenly, without any warning. Many boats have turned over in the rough waters.

On that special day, I walked with my brother David down to the lake. As we were skipping stones over the water, we saw Jesus with some of his disciples. We heard him say to Peter, "I'm so tired. Will you row me out to the middle of the lake in your boat so that I can get away from the crowds and sleep for a few hours?" Peter loved Jesus and would do anything for him. So you can guess what his answer was. "Of course I will, Jesus. Jump in." David and I watched until the boat was way out in the middle of the sea. Suddenly, rain clouds began to move across the sky. My brother and I ran back to our house. We didn't want to get soaked! I also wanted to make sure my pet goat would be tied up in a safe place.

> **Remember**
> Jesus is everywhere! I can always call on Jesus to help me whenever I am afraid.

David and I reached our home just before the rain started to pour. But the men who were out on the lake weren't so fortunate. This is what Philip, who was in the boat with Jesus and Peter, told us after the storm was over:

"By the time we reached the middle of the lake, Jesus was asleep on a cushion in the back of the boat. I looked up and watched dark clouds racing across the sky, right toward us! I said to Peter, 'We are going to have a big storm. Let's cover Jesus with my cloak so he won't get wet.' No sooner had we done that than heavy rain started to drench all of us. But Jesus stayed dry.

"Not only was it raining hard, but the winds were getting stronger and stronger. I was becoming really frightened. I had been out on the lake before in a storm, but nothing as bad as this. I knew I wasn't the only one who was afraid. I heard the others yelling and screaming as one huge wave after another splashed into our small boat. We held onto our seats so that we wouldn't be tossed out into the water, as one swell after another rocked our boat. I really thought we were going to sink or capsize. It was terrible. Amazingly, Jesus still didn't wake up.

> **Scripture Memory Verse**
>
> "Take heart, it is I; do not be afraid."
>
> (Mark 6:50)

"I didn't know what to do. But then I turned toward the back of the boat and saw Peter crawling over to Jesus. 'What are you doing, Peter?' I yelled. 'I'm going to wake Jesus,' he shouted back. I watched as he shook Jesus and said, 'Jesus, help us. We are about to drown.' Jesus knew our fear. He got to his feet, told the wind to die down, and said to the sea, 'Peace! Be still!' You'll never guess what happened. Immediately the water became calm. The dark clouds were blown away by a gentle breeze. Jesus looked at us all and said, 'Why were you so afraid? Have you still no faith?'

"We were so amazed! Can you imagine? Even the wind and the sea obey Jesus!"

Jesus, Speak to Me

I know what it is like to be afraid. I was afraid that night in the Garden of Gethsemane—the night before I was to die on the cross. But my heavenly Father gave me strength. He promised to be with me, just as I have promised to always be with you.

I asked my disciples why they had no faith. I was with them, and instead of being fearful, they should have trusted in me. But often it is hard to control our fears. Even some adults struggle with fear, and sometimes it keeps them from doing important things for me.

Is there something you fear? Do you know that I can heal you of your fears? When you pray to me, I will give you the trust and faith you need to let go of your fear.

Often it's helpful to tell someone what you are afraid of. Why don't you tell your mother or father what your fear is. They can pray with you. They can pray in my name to deliver you from your fear.

So the next time you feel afraid, call out to me, just like the disciples did. Imagine me standing right next to you. I'm so close to you. Maybe I'm even holding your hand.

Prayer

Jesus, I believe that you are everywhere. You are right here with me. You know everything that frightens me. Right now, Jesus, I ask you to heal me of . . . (name the fear).

The Parable of the Sower and the Seed

(Luke 8:4–8, 11–15)

I'm Rebekah, and here's a little quiz I want to give you. Do you remember what a parable is? I'll give you a clue. My brother David told you one the other day. Well, today I'm going to tell you another parable. This time Jesus used a farmer and seeds to bring his story to life.

My father had gone fishing very early one morning before the sun came up—that is the best time to catch fish, he always says. Both Jacob and David had gone with him. Father was hoping for a big catch so that there would be a lot of fish to sell when he got back to shore. When I woke up, my mom was busy sewing a patch on my father's tunic. Sarah had gone to get water from the well, so I was alone with Mother. It's fun having her all to myself. That's when I tell her everything that I'm thinking about, especially the things that worry me.

After we had chatted for a little while, Mother asked me if I would go down to the lake and wait for Father's boat to come in. She wanted me to bring home five large fish. She was planning to cook two fish that day. The other three she was going to salt and use later.

So off I went. It was a really clear day, with no haze, and I saw Father's boat still out in the middle of the lake. I thought to myself, "What will I do until the boat comes in?" It was then that I saw Jesus climbing into a boat. He spoke to the fisherman, who rowed him a little away from the shore. Then Jesus stood up in the boat and told this parable to the crowd that had gathered:

> **Remember**
>
> The words of Scripture can help me to live for Jesus if my heart is open and ready.

"A farmer got up one morning and said to himself, 'Now that the winter is over, it is time for me to plant seeds. Today, I will sow barley so that my wife can make bread for our family.' So the farmer went into his barn, picked up a large bag of seed, and went out into his field. Now he had just ploughed the field with his oxen, and the soil was ready for planting.

"But as the farmer was scattering the seeds, the wind blew, and some of the seeds fell on the path beside the field. Guess what happened? Some birds flew down and ate the seeds. What a great day for the birds!

"Some of the seeds that the farmer scattered fell onto rocky soil. The seeds sprouted quickly because the soil was not very deep. But as soon as the hot sun came out, the plants dried up and died, because they had not sunk deep roots into good soil.

"Some seeds fell in between thorns. The soil between the thorns was good, and the seeds sprouted. But the thorns began to choke the little plants, and they too died."

Jesus smiled and said, "But some of the seeds that the farmer scattered fell on good soil—with no rocks and no thorns. The seeds buried themselves in the soft soil, the rain watered them, and the sun helped them to germinate and grow. Every day, the farmer went to check what was happening in his field. First he saw the green shoots, then he saw the stalks, and finally he saw the grain. He was very happy. He went home and said to his wife, 'The seeds that landed on good soil have produced a great crop of a hundred times more than I scattered.' 'Oh, that is wonderful!' said his wife. 'We must thank God for a good harvest.'"

> **Scripture Memory Verse**
>
> "Let anyone with ears to hear listen!"
>
> (Luke 8:8)

Just as Jesus finished telling this parable, I saw my father's boat come to shore. We had delicious fish for dinner that night. I told everyone the parable about the sower and the seed, and we talked about what it could mean.

Jesus, Speak to Me

I hope you have used your imagination to picture the farmer scattering the seeds. Now I want you to imagine that the seeds are my teachings to you. Sometimes you hear one of my truths, but you don't pay attention to it. Then my teaching is like the seed that falls on the path. It never gets a chance to grow in you, because you never really give it much thought.

Other times you listen carefully to what I'm telling you, but you soon forget about it. Then my word is like the seed that falls on rocky soil. My teaching withers like the small plants, because it never gets deep enough into your heart.

And then there are times when you hear my truth in Scripture and really try to change your life. But you get so busy with other things that my teaching gets crowded out. That's when it's like the seed that grows among the thorns.

So what happens when you hear a truth from the Bible, and it lands on good soil in your heart? It can teach you, guide you, and encourage you. If it takes root in your heart, you will grow up to become a strong Christian, and you will be able to do so much for me. You will be able to build my kingdom here on earth!

During Lent, choose a Scripture verse and let it sink into your heart so that it will bear much fruit in your life. Repeat this verse to yourself every day.

Prayer

Jesus, thank you for your word in Scripture. Help me to have ears that will listen and a heart that will accept your truths.

A Family Journey with Jesus through Lent

Third Week
of Lent

week 3 | day 1

The Widow's Two Coins

(Luke 21:1–4; Matthew 22:17–22)

Guess what my name is? Here's a clue: I have the same name as Jesus' mother. That's right, my name is Mary! I'm twelve, and I live with my parents and grandmother in Nazareth. That's where Jesus lived with Mary and Joseph when he was growing up. When my mother and father were young, they both knew Jesus, because they lived in the same neighborhood.

My grandmother, who lives with us, is a widow. Her husband—my grandfather—died before I was born. In the mornings, my grandmother has been teaching me how to weave yarn into cloth and then sew it together to make clothes. Often while we are weaving and sewing, Grandma also tells me many stories about Jesus. Her favorite one is about the day when Mary and Joseph came back from Egypt with baby Jesus and settled here in Nazareth. I love listening to all of Grandma's stories about Jesus.

Now the story I'm going to tell you today is about a widow. But it's not about my grandmother! It's about a widow that Jesus saw in the Temple in Jerusalem. How do I know the story? Why, Grandma told me, of course!

After Jesus had chosen his disciples, he would often walk through the countryside from Capernaum to Jerusalem, which took about three or four days. But Jesus took the trip slowly, stopping along the way to heal all the sick people who were brought to him. At night, people would invite him to dinner and to stay in their homes. Often in the early morning, Jesus would get up and find a quiet spot to pray. He would praise and thank God for all the people that were being healed. He would also ask his Father what he was to do and say that day.

Remember

It pleases Jesus when I'm generous to others.

When Jesus got to Jerusalem, he often went to the Temple to speak to the chief priests, the teachers of the law, and the elders. One day they asked him, "Is it right to pay taxes to Caesar?" Jesus said, "Show me a coin. Whose head is on it?" They replied, "Caesar's." Jesus said, "Give to Caesar what is Caesar's, and to God what is God's."

But that's not all Jesus taught about money. One day, he saw rich people putting their money into the special Temple collection box. One after another they came to drop in their coins. Then Jesus saw a woman approaching the collection box. From the clothes that she wore, he could tell that she was a widow and that she was poor. She stopped, put her hand into her pocket, and took out two small copper coins. That was all the money she had. First she dropped one coin into the box. Then she put in her second coin. The widow gave both copper coins to God and didn't keep anything for herself.

Jesus was very surprised and pleased. He said to his disciples and all those around him, "Do you see this poor widow? She has put more into the collection box than all of the others." They looked at each other and asked, "What does Jesus mean?" He explained, "All the rich people gave just a little of what they had. They didn't give everything, because they didn't want to be without money. But this widow only had two coins, and yet she has given both of them. She has given God everything she has. She has been very generous today."

Scripture Memory Verse

"This poor widow has put in more than all of them."

(Luke 21:3)

My grandmother loves telling this story about the generous widow!

Jesus, Speak to Me

That poor widow gave everything she had to help others. She was so generous. She really trusted that God would take care of all of her needs.

There are different ways to be generous. You can serve me and help others by giving your time. Perhaps you can help your parents with a chore or volunteer with a project at your church. You can take some time to talk and listen to a relative or elderly neighbor who lives alone. Or, you can collect clothes, or food, or school supplies and give them to a charity that helps people who don't have enough. Also, I have given you gifts and talents, and you can share them with others. If you play a musical instrument, you might want to entertain the residents at a nursing home. And you can always share money you earn or part of your allowance with your parish or with someone in need.

I know that it's not always easy to be generous, especially if it means sacrificing your time or money. That's when it's good to remember the widow and how she trusted me with her life.

Spend a few minutes now talking as a family about how together you can perform an act of generosity for someone during Lent. Remember that when you serve others, you really are serving me.

Prayer

Father, I want to have a generous heart like the widow in today's story. Help me to trust you with my time, talents, and treasures so that I can freely give to others.

Jesus Heals the Ten Lepers

(Luke 17:11–19)

I'm Benjamin, and I'm nine years old. I was named after Jacob and Rachel's son, who we read about in the Torah. Judith, my sister, is eleven. My father owns a vineyard just outside of Jerusalem. When harvest time comes, Judith and I go down to the vineyard to help Father pick the grapes. It's very hard work, but Father makes it fun for us. The first to fill his or her basket gets to eat a big handful. I've won many times!

When all the grapes have been picked, Father loads the baskets onto our donkey and heads for the market in Jerusalem. Sometimes I go with him. We enter Jerusalem through one of the gates in the city's walls. Often some beggars are sitting by the gates. We then walk through the narrow streets to a market where Father knows he will find some merchants. They are always pleased to buy his fresh, juicy grapes to make into wine.

When Father returned from the market last week, he was so excited. He told us that Jesus had healed ten lepers. His story was so amazing! But first, let me tell you about lepers.

People who are called "lepers" have a terrible disease that makes the skin on their ears, nose, fingers, and toes very, very sore. Children as well as grownups can get this disease, which is called leprosy. The really sad thing about leprosy is that you never get better from it. Also, it spreads easily from one person to another. You can imagine that everyone is very frightened of getting leprosy.

> **Remember**
>
> When I say thank you, it shows that I am grateful for what has been given to me.

Because no one wants to be near lepers, they are forced to live in caves outside the city. It is very difficult when a mother or father gets leprosy, because they have to leave their home and children and live with the other lepers. Some people take food to the lepers. They call out that they are leaving a basket for them, and the lepers don't come out until the people have gone away. Sometimes, when lepers come into the city, they ring a bell and cry out, "Unclean, unclean." This is a warning for people to run in the opposite direction.

This is the story that my father told us: One day ten men who had leprosy heard that Jesus—who was on his way to Jerusalem—was passing through a village near their caves. They had heard all about Jesus and how he healed people. So they thought to themselves, "Let's go and ask Jesus to make us better." They crouched down behind some trees, waiting for him. They hid, because if anyone saw them, they would have to go back to their caves. They waited and waited, and then they heard the crowd shouting, "Here comes Jesus!" One of the lepers said, "We shouldn't get too near him." So they decided to come out from behind their trees and call to him from there. In really loud voices they called, "Jesus, Master, have mercy on us!"

Scripture Memory Verse

"Give thanks to the LORD, for he is good; his steadfast love endures forever."

(Psalm 118:1)

Do you think that Jesus said, "Don't come any closer"? No, Jesus wasn't afraid. He prayed to his heavenly Father and said, "Dear lepers, go into the city and show yourselves to the priest." Guess what? As they started to walk along the path, they were healed. The sores went away, and their skin became soft again. Oh, they were so happy and excited! Now they didn't have to live in caves any longer. They could go back home to their families.

But that's not the end of the story. This is the best part. One of the lepers, who was from a foreign country, turned around and ran back to Jesus and fell at his feet. "Oh, Jesus," he cried out, "thank you so much for healing me!" Jesus looked at him and said, "I'm so glad that you have come back to thank me. But where are the other nine lepers that I healed? Why didn't they come back with you?" Then Jesus took the man by the hand and said, "Get up and go on your way. Your faith has made you well."

Jesus, Speak to Me

Thank you for reading another story about my life today. When you say these two words—"thank you"—you show that your heart is grateful for what has been done for you.

But do you sometimes forget to say thank you? As you read in the story today, nine out of the ten men with leprosy forgot to come back and thank me for healing them. But one remembered, and he praised God because he had been cured.

Prayer

Father, you have given so much to me. Please help me to be grateful.

What are some ways this Lent that you can grow in gratitude? Perhaps everyone in your family can take turns saying the prayer of thanksgiving before meals. Remember especially to thank your mom and dad for all that they do for you. And when you say your prayers at night, thank your Father in heaven for something he did for you that day.

When we remember to thank our Father for all that he has given us, it makes us love him even more! Right now, why don't you take turns with other members of your family and thank God for one or two things he has done for you.

week 3 | day 3

The Transfiguration of Jesus

(Matthew 17:1–13; Luke 9:28–36)

It's David here again to tell you another story about Jesus. I heard it one evening as I was sitting outside with my friend Aaron and his father, who is a tanner. Tanners make the leather that is used for belts, straps, and buckets—and even for the sandals of Roman soldiers. As we were watching the sun go down behind the hills, I asked Aaron's dad how he makes leather.

First, he explained, he gets the skin of an animal, such as a cow, a goat, or a sheep. Next he scrapes the hair and fat from the skin using a tool made from an animal bone. After that he soaks the skin in lime and juices of plants to soften it. He says that the mixture smells really bad, so the tanners work far away from any houses! Finally he lays the skin out in the sun to dry. Then the leather is ready to be cut and sewed.

My questions had just been answered when along came James, one of Jesus' disciples, who was visiting his family here in Capernaum. I heard him say to some of our neighbors, "Come and sit down. Now that Jesus has risen from the dead, I want to tell you what happened one day when Peter, John, and I were with Jesus." When I heard the name Jesus, I asked, "Can we come and listen, too?" James smiled and said, "Oh yes! Come and sit down."

James began his story: "I loved being with Jesus. It was such a privilege to be one of his twelve disciples. My brother, John, was also one of his special friends. Jesus taught us how to pray. He also helped us to get along with one another. He told us to love and to forgive those who have hurt us. Even when Jesus had to correct us, he was always very kind and understanding.

> **Remember**
> Jesus is both God and man. His glory was revealed to three of his disciples at the Transfiguration.

"Sometimes Jesus would say, 'I'm tired. Let's get away from the crowds so that I can rest.' One day Jesus took Peter, John, and me to a very high mountain. I thought to myself, 'Jesus must be tired. He wants to rest.' But when we got to the top of the mountain, Jesus didn't rest, but started to pray. Then it happened—Jesus began to glow! His face shone so brightly that it looked like the sun. And his clothes became a dazzling white. I couldn't take my eyes off him.

"Two men appeared with him. Guess who they were? Moses and Elijah! They started talking to Jesus, but I couldn't hear what they were saying. Now, remember that Moses and Elijah lived a long, long time ago—but there they were, standing with Jesus! I was so surprised that I couldn't say anything. But Peter did!

"Peter, who was really excited, stood up and said, 'Jesus, would you like me to build three tents—one for you, one for Moses, and one for Elijah?' He thought that if they were going to stay there, they would be more comfortable if they had tents to shade them. But just as he was saying this, a bright cloud covered all of us, and a voice said, 'This is my Son, the Beloved; with him I am well pleased. Listen to him.'

"I was so shocked and afraid that I fell flat on the ground and hid my face in my hands. I looked to the side and saw that Peter and John had done the same thing! I don't know how long we stayed like that, but finally Jesus came over and touched us and said, 'Get up. Don't be afraid.' When I looked up, Jesus was alone. Moses and Elijah were gone.

> **Scripture Memory Verse**
>
> "And the Word became flesh and lived among us, and we have seen his glory."
>
> (John 1:14)

"Then it was time to leave the mountain. As we walked down the winding path, Jesus told us not to tell anyone what we had seen until he had risen from the dead."

When James had finished his story, we all asked him questions about this extraordinary day in the life of Jesus!

Jesus, Speak to Me

Some things that you see or hear are easy to understand. But when my appearance on the mountain was changed, the disciples had a hard time grasping what was happening. The disciples saw my heavenly glory. They usually saw me as a man, but I was also God.

How the disciples saw me on that special day is how I am now in heaven. I have a glorified body. When I walked the earth, people saw a little bit of my glory when I performed a miracle. Mostly, however, my glory was hidden. Now I reign in heaven in my full glory. It will be so wonderful when you are with me in heaven!

If you look carefully, you can still see my glory on earth. You can see it in the lives of the saints. You can see it when a prayer is miraculously answered. You can see it in the beauty of creation. Talk about my glory with your family. Where do you see it?

Prayer

Jesus, you are the Son of God. I want to see you someday in your glory in heaven!

The Woman at the Well

(John 4:1–41)

I hope you are looking forward to today's story about Jesus! We haven't met before. I'm Leah. My sister, Hannah, told you about Jesus' forty days in the desert. Sometimes in the early mornings, I climb the outside stairs to our roof so that I can watch the sun rise over the lake. It's amazing to see that big red ball climb up into the sky! Tiberias is a busy town, but at that time of the morning it's so peaceful and quiet. The only sounds you can hear are the songs of the birds and the distant whistle of the shepherds calling their sheep.

Another thing I enjoy is going to the well for our drinking and cooking water. I either take a goatskin bucket or a jar. I've learned to balance the jar on my head like my mother and the other women do. At the well I usually meet with some of my friends.

Mother often says that I can stay a while and play before coming home. But often, instead of playing, my friends and I listen as the women share their stories about Jesus. As they drop their empty buckets into the well and draw out clean, cold water, the women enjoy chatting with one another. The story I'm going to tell you today is about a woman who met Jesus at a well.

Jesus loved walking around the countryside, teaching the people and healing all who were sick. He walked to the North, the South, the East, and the West. One day when he was walking from the South to the North—heading back to the Sea of Galilee—his journey took him through Samaria, where there are some large mountains. This is where the Samaritans live.

> **Remember**
>
> Jesus wants me to share the good news about him with my friends.

It was about noon when Jesus said to his disciples, "Let's stop and eat lunch here in this town. We have walked all morning in the hot sun. I'm tired and hungry. How about you?" Everyone agreed that it was time to rest and eat. Peter said, "Jesus, over there is the well. Why don't you sit there and rest, while we go and buy food." The disciples left, and Jesus sat down by the well, which was on the land that Jacob had given to his son Joseph. Do you remember the story of Jacob, who gave his son Joseph a coat of many colors?

Jesus had been sitting at the well only a little while when a woman came to get water. Jesus said to her, "Please give me a drink." The woman was really surprised and said, "You want me to give you a drink? You're Jewish and I'm Samaritan. Jews and Samaritans don't like each other. We don't even eat together." Jesus looked at her and said, "If you knew who I really am, you would have asked me for living water."

"Living water!" said the woman. "Where can you get that? You don't even have a bucket to drop into this well where our father Jacob, his sons, and his flocks used to drink." Jesus replied, "Everyone who drinks this water will be thirsty again. But whoever drinks the water that I will give will have eternal life." Now, the woman didn't understand that eternal life meant living with Jesus forever in heaven. So she replied, "Oh, please give me that water. Then I won't have to keep coming here to this well."

Scripture Memory Verse

"Out of the believer's heart shall flow rivers of living water." (John 7:38)

Jesus and the woman talked about many other things. The woman was surprised that Jesus knew so much about her life, even though they had just met. It made her think that he might be the Messiah. Then Jesus said, "I am he, the one who is speaking to you."

Just then the disciples came back with the food they had bought. They were really surprised to see Jesus and the woman talking together. The woman was so excited about Jesus that she left her water jar and went back to the city. She told everyone about him. She said, "He told me everything I have ever done." Many Samaritans believed that Jesus was the Savior of the world because of what this woman had said.

Jesus, Speak to Me

It's always fun telling others good news. That's what I did for three years. I told people that their Father in heaven loved them, that they could repent of their sins, and that they could live forever with my Father and me in heaven. The Samaritan woman also told her family and friends the good news about meeting me.

Do you have any good news to share with someone? How about good news about me and what I've done for you? What about a prayer I answered, or how I healed you of a fear? What are some of the things about my life that you would like to tell others? Perhaps you could speak to them about my love for them, how I died for them, and how I want to be their friend forever.

> **Prayer**
>
> Jesus, you are the good news! Please fill me with your Holy Spirit and help me to tell others about you.

During Lent, perhaps you can say to someone, "I would like to tell you about my friend, Jesus." Share with them something that I have done in your life.

week 3 | day 5

Martha and Mary

(Luke 10:38–42)

You are now in Bethany, in Judea. It's a town about two miles southeast of Jerusalem and not too far from Bethlehem, where Jesus was born. And who am I? My name is Rachel, and I'm eight. My brother, Reuben, is ten. Both of us are named after people in Jacob's family. Rachel was Jacob's wife, and Reuben was the oldest of his children.

When Jesus came to Jerusalem with his disciples, he would often stay here in Bethany with his friends, Martha, Mary, and Lazarus. My brother and I often have fun listening to people from Galilee, like Peter and Jesus' other disciples, because their accents are different from ours. Do you ever try to guess where people live by listening to their accents?

I would like to tell you about the day that Jesus made a surprise visit to Bethany. I was out picking some colorful wildflowers for my mother. I had a big bunch in my hand when I heard some of our neighbors calling out, "Jesus is back!" Jesus was very popular, and everyone was excited when he visited Bethany.

It was about the sixth hour (that's three o'clock in the afternoon) when Jesus arrived. Among those who rushed out to greet him were Martha, Mary, and Lazarus. I heard Martha say, "Jesus, are you coming to our home for dinner today?" "Martha, I would love to," he replied. So Martha disappeared! Where did she go? Here's what Martha told my mother:

> **Remember**
> Jesus wants me to slow down and choose a time every day to be with him in prayer.

"I was so thrilled that Jesus was coming to have dinner at our home. He is such a special guest, and we love having him with us. Usually I plan ahead for guests, but Jesus took us by surprise. So I had lots of things to do to get ready for dinner. I said to myself, 'Oh, I'm so glad that Mary will be able to help me.'

"First I ran up to the roof to get some dry wood to start a fire in the oven. The floor hadn't been swept that day, so that was the next job. I had just finished sweeping when in walked Jesus. 'Jesus, I'm so glad to see you. Please sit. I'll bring you some water,' I said, rushing off to get it. I didn't even stop to give Jesus a hug. When I got back with the water, Jesus was talking to Mary. 'I'm happy Mary is talking to Jesus,' I said to myself.

"I started to make some bread. When the dough was ready, I popped it into the oven. Mary was still talking to Jesus. I began to complain to myself, 'Mary's not helping me. Doesn't she know I've got a lot to do?' To prepare the fish stew, I ran outside and picked some fresh herbs, and then I went to the box where we keep the salted fish. 'Oh, where's Mary? I thought to myself. 'I need her here. Why is she spending all this time talking to Jesus?'

"'Mary, I need your help,' I said in a loud voice across the room, where she was sitting at Jesus' feet. But Mary didn't seem to hear me. 'Mary, I really want you to come here right now,' I said even more loudly. I was getting really angry! I decided to go over and talk to Jesus. I needed him on my side! 'Jesus, don't you think that Mary should come and help me get dinner ready?' I asked.

Scripture Memory Verse

"Mary has chosen the better part, which will not be taken away from her."

(Luke 10:42)

"Jesus looked at me so kindly and said, 'Martha, thank you for preparing dinner for us. But please don't be angry with Mary. You are worried and distracted by many things.' Then he said something that really surprised me. 'Martha, it's good that Mary is talking to me. She has made the better choice.'

"Suddenly, I wasn't angry with Mary any longer. The truth of the words that Jesus spoke to me changed my heart. I saw everything from a different perspective. Yes! Mary had chosen to sit and listen to Jesus. It wasn't that she didn't want to help me, but she had to make a choice—and I saw now that it was a very good choice.

"Are you wondering about what happened with dinner? I finished preparing the rest of the meal very quickly. As we sat down at the table, Jesus gave me a big smile before he said the prayer of thanksgiving."

Jesus, Speak to Me

I always enjoyed spending evenings with my good friends Martha, Mary, and Lazarus. They all loved me very much and showed their love in different ways.

One way that you can show your love for me is by sitting at my feet like Mary did. I know you are busy, but it really pleases me when you make a choice to be with me for a few minutes each day.

Talk with your mom and dad about choosing a place in your home to set up a "prayer corner." What would you want to put in it? Perhaps you'd like a picture of me, or a crucifix, or some flowers. In your prayer time you can talk to me, read the Bible, pray the rosary, sing songs, or just sit quietly in my presence.

Prayer

Jesus, I want to spend time with you every day. Help me to take a few minutes with you, no matter how busy I am.

Lent

The Parable of the Prodigal Son

(Luke 15:11–32)

Welcome back to Jericho. I'm Samuel. My father is a farmer who owns some land outside the city walls, and I'm his helper. When it's time to get the soil ready for planting, we borrow a wooden plough and oxen from a neighboring farmer. Once the fields are plowed, I walk up and down each row scattering the barley or wheat seeds, which I carry in a big sack over my shoulders. It's a long and tiring job. As the months go by, Father and I go out into the fields to see what's growing. If we see any large weeds growing in between the young shoots, we pull them out. Finally the grain is ripe and ready to be cut. With a sickle we chop it down and tie it into sheaves.

One day when we were standing in the fields, Father remembered a parable Jesus told about a farmer. Here's the story Jesus told:

"There once was a rich farmer who had two sons. Both of them worked on their father's farm. The older son was a good worker and did everything that his father asked him to do. But the younger son wasn't very happy. He kept complaining, 'I don't like doing all this hard work. I want to go away and have some fun.' Then he had an idea. He went into the house and asked, 'Father, would you give me my share of the money that will be mine one day?' His father was sad, but he replied, 'Son, if that is what you want, here it is.'

"Oh, the younger son was so happy! He quickly packed his things, and off he went. After days of walking, he arrived in a new country. He said to himself, 'This is going to be so much fun!' He bought some new clothes. Then he went to the market and spent lots of his money on food and drink and threw a big party for his new friends. Everyone knew that this stranger had a great deal of money. 'We really like you,' they said. 'Can we come here for another party tomorrow?' So every day he went out and spent a lot of his money.

> **Remember**
>
> My heavenly Father loves me and is always ready to welcome me back. No sin is too big to be forgiven. Jesus has died for all of my sins.

"One day when the younger son counted his money, he found that he only had enough left to buy a loaf of bread. So he went to his new friends and said, 'I've invited you to many meals at my house. Now that I have no money left, may I come to your house?' 'No!' they said. 'Go away. We don't want to be your friends anymore.' So he went away. That day he only had bread to eat. The next day, he had nothing to eat, but again, his friends refused to give him anything. So he decided to find a job. He asked many people if they would give him work.

"At last a farmer told the younger son that he could take care of the pigs. It was a very dirty job, and he didn't like it. But at least he had something to eat. Can you guess what he ate? The pigs' food! One day when he was cleaning out the pigpen, he thought, 'What am I doing here? I'm so sad and lonely. I want to go home.' So off he went. On the way he thought about what he would say to his father: 'Father, I'm sorry for leaving you. I've done many things wrong since I left home. I want to come back. But I don't deserve to be your son anymore. I will be one of your servants.'

Scripture Memory Verse

"This son of mine was dead and is alive again; he was lost and is found!"

(Luke 15:24)

"All the time that the younger son was away, his father had missed him very much. Every day he would scan the road, hoping to see him returning. Then one day, in the distance, the father spotted someone walking toward him. 'Could this be my son?' he wondered. 'It is!' he exclaimed. He ran toward his son and hugged him and kissed him. He was so happy to see him again! The son said, 'Father, forgive me. Let me come back and be one of your servants.' But instead of answering him, the father called out, 'Servants, go and get new clothes and sandals for my son. Bring one of my golden rings. Let's have a party to celebrate. My son has come back to me!'"

Jesus, Speak to Me

Close your eyes and try to imagine the father in this parable running out to his younger son and giving him a big hug! Just like that father, I want you to know that my heavenly Father is so happy when you go to him in prayer and ask him to forgive you for the things you have done wrong. You can do this every night. Before you go to sleep, you can ask for your Father's forgiveness and say the Act of Contrition.

If you've already made your first Penance, come to me this Lent in the Sacrament of Reconciliation. I'm waiting for you. Tell me everything. Don't be afraid or ashamed. When the priest gives you absolution, know that I have forgiven all of your sins, and that the angels are rejoicing in heaven! I want to pour out so many graces on you through this wonderful sacrament.

Prayer

Jesus, I thank you for the Sacrament of Reconciliation. Holy Spirit, help me to make a good confession.

A Family Journey with Jesus through Lent

Fourth Week
of Lent

week 4 | day 1

Jesus Heals Jairus' Daughter

(Luke 8:40–56)

Welcome back to Capernaum. I'm Sarah. Today I have some news for you. We have a new baby goat at our house. He's so cute! My twin brother, Jacob, and I have decided to call it Kid! Now we have three goats: King, Sheba, and Kid. Everyone in my family loves animals, especially our father. When the neighbors have a sick or injured animal, Father shows them how to care for it.

Father's job is making and repairing fishing boats. He made the boats that belong to Peter and some of Jesus' other disciples. It's great to think that Jesus travels from place to place in one of my father's boats! When Father is really busy, he doesn't come home for lunch, so I take food to the lake for him.

That brings me to my story. I was heading to the lake with Father's lunch one afternoon when I saw a crowd of people gathering along the shore. "What's happening?" I asked. One of the women said, "We're waiting for Jesus." Another said, "Look! There he is in the boat with the big sail." I quickly found my father and gave him his food. Then I stood on a high rock so I could get a good view of Jesus as he came to shore.

Everyone cheered as Jesus got out of the boat. Suddenly I saw a man pushing his way through the crowd. He was shouting, "I need to talk to Jesus." It was Jairus, the ruler of our synagogue. When he reached Jesus, Jairus threw himself on the ground. "Jesus, please help me!" he sobbed. "My little daughter is very sick. I'm afraid she's going to die." Jesus took Jairus' arm and said, "Take me to her."

As the crowd of people followed Jesus and Jairus on the way to his house, I saw a woman creep up from behind and touch the hem of Jesus' cloak. Jesus stopped and said, "Who touched me?" His disciple Peter replied, "What do you mean, Jesus? There are so many people who are pressing in on you." But Jesus said, "Someone touched me because I noticed that power has gone out from me." Then a woman came out of the crowd, trembling. "I was sick, Jesus. I spent all my money on doctors, but no one could make me better. But when I touched your cloak, I was healed." Jesus said, "Daughter, your faith has made you well. Go in peace."

Just then a messenger from Jairus' house ran out to meet him. He looked very sad as he said, "Jairus, your daughter is dead. Don't trouble Jesus any longer. It's too late." Jairus fell to his knees, sobbing. Jesus put his arm around him and whispered, "Don't be afraid, Jairus. Believe in me, and your daughter will live."

> **Remember**
>
> Jesus has given us the Sacrament of the Anointing of the Sick. I can reach out and touch the hem of Jesus' cloak every day and ask to be healed, protected, or helped.

As we got closer to Jairus' house, I heard the wailing sound of reed pipes, which are played when people die. I also saw people crying. Jesus said, "Don't cry. The little girl is only sleeping." Turning toward Jairus, he said, "Would you and your wife please take me to see your daughter?" Jesus nodded to Peter, James, and John. They went into the house with him.

> **Scripture Memory Verse**
>
> "Your faith has made you well."
>
> (Luke 8:48)

After a few minutes, Jairus came outside and exclaimed, "My daughter is alive! Jesus has healed her!" "What happened?" a woman in the crowd asked. Jairus said, "Jesus took her hand and said, 'Little girl, get up.' She immediately sat up! Then he told us to give her something to eat."

Jairus was overjoyed. "Jesus has performed a miracle for my family today!"

Jesus, Speak to Me

In this story you heard about how I healed two people. I want you to know that I still heal people today. One of the ways I heal people is through the Sacrament of the Anointing of the Sick. People's souls are always healed from this sacrament, and sometimes their bodies are healed as well.

Do you and your family ever pray for healing for one another? If your brother or sister has a headache, a sore throat, or a stomachache, take his or her hand and say a short, simple prayer, asking me to heal them. It pleases me when you do this, because you show both your love and concern for one another and your faith in me. And don't be surprised if the pain goes away! But even if it doesn't, know that I still love you and want you to come to me when you are suffering. Remember, I am always with you.

Prayer

Jesus, I believe in you. I ask that you heal all those who are sick. I especially ask for healing for . . . (name a particular person).

week 4 | day 2

A Woman Pours Perfume on Jesus' Feet

(Luke 7:36–50)

I'm Reuben, the brother of Rachel. Do you remember where we live? I'll give you a hint—our town is only two miles from Jerusalem. You're right, it's Bethany! Today I'd like to tell you about the Temple in Jerusalem. The first one was built by King Solomon. But the Babylonians, who were enemies of Israel, destroyed it and made our people leave Jerusalem. When the Hebrews came back to Jerusalem seventy years later, they rebuilt the Temple. It's not as beautiful and grand as the first one, but it's still a very special place.

Jewish people love to go to the Temple to pray and to worship God. It's always a busy place! We try to follow the Law of Moses. A group of men called the Pharisees help us to do that by teaching us and interpreting God's commandments for us.

My aunt works for a Pharisee called Simon, who lives in Bethany. Whenever he has guests for dinner, she has to help with the cooking and the serving. She told Rachel and me that one day Simon invited Jesus to dinner. My aunt loves Jesus very much, so you can imagine how excited she was about this special guest. Here's what she told me:

"Jesus arrived at Simon's house late in the afternoon. He had been walking all day in the hot sun. His feet were dirty and sore when he arrived. Simon was so pleased when Jesus arrived, and he had so many questions to ask him, that he forgot to ask his servants to get a basin of water to wash Jesus' feet. The other servants and I had made a wonderful dinner—roasted meats, vegetables, breads, and fruit—and when Simon gave us the sign, we began putting the food on the big table.

> **Remember**
>
> My heavenly Father is so merciful.

"Simon's neighbors had spotted Jesus when he arrived, and they told their friends, who told *their* friends. Everyone was excited that Jesus was back in Bethany. Many people were crowding around the door of Simon's house and peeking through the windows. Somehow a woman in the crowd managed to sneak into the house. She fell down at Jesus' feet. Some of Simon's Pharisee friends said, 'Oh no!' You see, they knew that this woman had done many bad things. They thought, 'Jesus won't want this woman near him.'

"Suddenly the woman started crying. Her tears fell on Jesus' feet. With her long dark hair, she wiped them dry. Next she gently kissed one foot and then the other. I heard her say very quietly, 'Oh Jesus, I am sorry for all the bad choices I have made. I am so sorry for all the wrong things I have done.' Wrapped in her shawl, she had a beautiful jar filled with very expensive perfume. She took it out, broke off the top, and poured all the oily perfume over Jesus' feet. It smelled wonderful!

"But Simon thought, 'Why is Jesus letting this woman touch him? She's a sinner.' Jesus knew what he was thinking. 'Simon, I have something to tell you,' Jesus said. 'There was a rich man who lent money to two different men. To one man he lent a great deal of money, and to the other, just a small amount. Neither of the two men was able to pay him back, so he cancelled their debt and told them they no longer owed him anything. Who do you think loved the rich man more?' Simon answered, 'The man who owed the most money!' 'You're right,' said Jesus.

> **Scripture Memory Verse**
>
> "Her sins, which were many, have been forgiven; hence she has shown great love."
>
> (Luke 7:47)

"'Listen carefully to what I'm going to say to you,' said Jesus. 'When I came to your house today, you didn't give me any water to wash my feet, and you didn't greet me with a kiss. But this woman bathed my feet with her tears and kissed my feet. She is now showing me how much she loves me because her many sins have been forgiven.'

"Jesus took the woman's hands and said, 'Your sins are forgiven. Your faith has saved you. Now go in peace.'"

How happy that woman must have been that day!

Jesus, Speak to Me

The woman who bathed my feet in her tears really loved me. She knew that my Father had sent me to tell everyone that their sins were forgiven. She was so happy to be forgiven! She was like the man who suddenly found out that he didn't have to repay his large debt. He was free of it, just as this woman was free of her sins.

Simon the Pharisee had trouble understanding why I would want to be close to sinners. That's because he didn't understand my Father's mercy. His mercy is so great that when we say we are sorry, he always forgives whatever sin we bring to him.

Prayer

Father, may everyone come to know your merciful love.

In the world today there are men and women who don't know about my Father's mercy. Many people who have committed serious crimes don't know that my Father would forgive them if they came to him. Think about someone who's been in the news lately who's done something very wrong. Right now pray the "Our Father" for this person. Pray that he or she will discover the merciful love of my Father.

Jesus Feeds the Five Thousand

(Mark 6:30–44; John 6:1–15)

I'm so glad you're here today with Rebekah, David, Sarah, and me in Capernaum. I'm Jacob, and I'm going to tell you about the time I spoke to Jesus! What started out as an ordinary day ended up being very extraordinary.

David and I had gone to school at the synagogue. I've been going to synagogue school since I was six. We study the Torah. "Torah" is the Hebrew word for instruction. As well as studying Scripture, we learn all about where and how people lived long ago. I love going to school. I hope that one day I'll be able to go to the Temple in Jerusalem to sit at the feet of a learned rabbi.

When we came out of the synagogue, I overheard some of the teachers saying that Jesus had been seen in a boat on the Sea of Galilee. I was very excited to hear this news, and I wondered where his boat would land. I really wanted to see him again. So I ran home as fast as I could. "Mother," I said, "Jesus is out on the lake. When his boat lands, David, Sarah, and I want to see him. May we go, please?" "Yes," Mother replied. "But you must take your lunches with you. You won't be able to buy food there." She quickly wrapped up five barley loaves and two salted fish. "I'm in charge of lunch," I said, as I gave my mother a kiss good-bye.

The first one out of the house was Sarah. She ran up the slope behind our house. "I can see a boat nearing the shore," she said. "That must be Jesus'." We ran quite a way to the spot where the boat had been tied up. By that time, a huge crowd had gathered around Jesus to listen to his teachings. It was really hot sitting in the sun, but I didn't mind because I was with Jesus.

> **Remember**
>
> Jesus has given himself to us in the Eucharist. He is truly present to us.

Just as the sun was going down over the hills, I heard Philip, one of Jesus' disciples, say to him, "Master, it's getting late. Shouldn't we tell the people to go to a nearby town to buy food? This is a lonely place. There's nowhere to buy anything on this side of the lake." "Philip," Jesus replied, "don't send them away. You give them something to eat." "What? Feed them myself?" Philip asked with surprise. "All the money I could earn in six months wouldn't be enough to buy food for all these thousands of people."

I opened up my own bundle of food, and was just about to give a piece of bread and fish to David and Sarah, when one of Jesus' disciples spoke to me. "My name is Andrew," he said. "What do you have there?" "Five barley loaves and two salted fish," I replied. Andrew thought for a moment and said, "Please bring your food and come with me." I jumped up and followed Andrew. The next thing I knew, I was standing in front of Jesus. Andrew whispered to Jesus,

"There's a boy here with five barley loaves and two salted fish, but that won't feed this huge crowd." Jesus looked at me and said, "Hello! Would you like to share your food with all of these people?" "Oh yes! Please take all of it," I said.

> ## Scripture Memory Verse
>
> "I am the living bread that came down from heaven. Whoever eats of this bread will live forever."
>
> (John 6:51)

Jesus took my food and put it in a basket. Next he told everyone to sit down in groups of fifty. I counted a hundred groups—five thousand people! Then he took the basket of food, lifted it up to heaven, and blessed and broke the loaves. He told his disciples to start handing out the food. They took out the fish and loaves, and then more fish and loaves, and then even more fish and loaves. The basket was never empty! Everyone had enough to eat. There were even twelve baskets of leftovers!

All the way home, I had to pinch myself. I thought, "Today, I've seen a real miracle by my friend Jesus."

Jesus, Speak to Me

When I fed those hungry people, I left them with a memory of just how much I cared about them. But I have given you more than a memory of my love and care—I have given you myself! Every time you receive the Eucharist at Mass, you are receiving me. I love coming to you. I love being so close to you! When you receive me in the Eucharist, we are the closest we can be to each other until you someday join me in heaven.

Please talk to me after you've received Holy Communion. I love hearing you say, "I love you, Jesus. Thank you for coming to earth, for teaching me, for sending me your Holy Spirit, and for giving me eternal life. I give my life to you." Also, tell me what you would like me to do for you. Perhaps there is someone you would like me to heal, help, or comfort. Ask me questions about who I am. Don't forget to listen to what I have to say to you!

During Lent, perhaps you can try to go to Mass twice a week—on Sunday and on another day, such as Saturday morning.

Prayer

Jesus, I praise you for becoming our heavenly bread. Please help me to always be respectful and reverent of you in the Eucharist.

The Parable of the Hidden Treasure

(Matthew 13:44)

I'd like to tell you another of my grandmother's stories about Jesus. So, can you guess who I am? I'm Mary. Welcome back to Nazareth! Do you remember that my grandmother is teaching me to weave? Whenever she is asked to make a cloak—the outer garment that men wear—she has to go to the busy, noisy market to buy the wool. Once back home, Grandma is very quick at stretching the yarn from the top hooks of her loom to the bottom ones. This yarn is called the warp. She lets me pass the wooden shuttle full of wool over and under the warp threads, from one side of the loom to the other. The wool that goes from side to side is called the weft.

When she has woven two pieces of cloth, she sews them together to make the cloak. Grandma told me that Jesus had a cloak that was seamless. It was made out of one piece of cloth, which must have been woven on a very large loom. I wonder who gave Jesus that special cloak.

My grandmother knew many of Jesus' parables from hearing them repeated at the market. She said people understood the kingdom of God better when Jesus taught in parables. This is Jesus' story about hidden treasure:

> **Remember**
>
> Jesus wants me to make him "number one" in my life!

"Early one morning a man called Mark said good-bye to his wife and three children and left to visit his elderly mother in another town. He crossed a neighbor's field that was lying fallow that year. Every seventh year, farmers let the soil in a field rest and don't grow any crops there. As Mark was walking along, whistling to himself, he suddenly stumbled. 'Did I trip over a rock?' he asked himself. As he bent down to fix his sandal, he was surprised to discover not a rock, but a box that was half buried in the soil.

"Mark had to work hard to pull the box out of the soil, because it was quite heavy. It was locked, so he picked up a stone and hit the lock really hard. When the lid popped open, Mark couldn't believe what he saw! The box was full of treasure—gold coins, cups, vases, and jewelry. 'Wow!' said Mark, jumping for joy. 'If I owned this field, I would be very rich.'

"'I need a plan! I need to buy this field,' he thought. So he buried the treasure again and ran back home. Lydia, his wife, saw him coming and cried out, 'What happened, Mark? Are you sick?' 'No! I found some hidden treasure in a field,' he whispered. 'I've got to sell everything we own so that we can buy the field. Then we'll be rich.' Lydia nearly fainted! 'Sell everything?' she gulped.

Scripture Memory Verse

"The kingdom of heaven is like treasure hidden in a field."

(Matthew 13:44)

"So they piled everything they owned onto the back of their poor little donkey: bundles of clothes, bed rolls, baskets of food, water pitchers, cooking pots, stools, and even a table. Lydia gave Mark the money she was going to use that day to buy food. Mark went to the market and sold everything. He also sold his house. People were getting very curious! Just as the sun was going down, he sold his donkey. Now he didn't own a thing. But his money bag was full.

"Mark rushed off to the home of the owner of the field. 'I'd like to buy your field that is fallow this year. Will you sell it to me, please?' 'Let me think about it,' said the farmer. Mark held up his money bag. 'I'll give you all this money,' he said. 'Sold!' said the farmer. They shook hands in agreement. Lydia was waiting for Mark as he came out of the house. 'Did you buy the field?' she asked. 'Yes!' replied Mark. 'Now let's go and dig up the treasure.'"

What's the meaning behind this story? According to my grandmother, Jesus told everyone that this is what finding the kingdom of heaven is like. It's so valuable that we would sell everything we own just to have it. But the good news is that it doesn't come with a price tag! Jesus said that we just need to have faith in him. Then the kingdom of heaven will be ours!

Jesus, Speak to Me

Can you think of anyone who has staked all his time, energy, and money on one goal? Perhaps you have heard about Olympic champions who wanted to win the gold medal so much that they spent all their time and energy practicing and all their money on coaches and competitions. They had to leave other interests behind in order to concentrate all their efforts on that one goal.

It really pleases me when people say, "My goal is to know Jesus and to tell others about him!" Then I know that I have become the greatest treasure in their lives! Can you think of people—past and present—who have made me their greatest treasure? How about Blessed Mother Teresa or Pope John Paul II? Perhaps you can read about what others have done to build my kingdom on earth. What about people you know personally, like your parish priest?

Prayer

Father, thy kingdom come, thy will be done, on earth as it is in heaven.

Jesus Walks on Water

(Matthew 14:22–33; Mark 6:45–52)

I've waited a long time to tell you my story! I'm Daniel, the brother of Hannah and Leah. As a boy, my father loved reading about Daniel's faith and courage in the lion's den. So when I was born, he named me after his hero!

Father is a tailor, which means that he makes clothes. Just last week three people came to Father's market stall. One man wanted two simple tunics for his children and one for himself. A woman asked him to sew an elaborate, colorful garment for her to wear to her son's wedding. And Father was particularly honored that a rabbi asked him to sew him a blue-fringed robe.

So Father is really busy right now. But every evening he takes time to ask us about our day. Father will often ask if we've been kind to one another. Yesterday he told us that we must forgive each other seventy times seven times. I thought that was a lot! But Father said that's what Jesus taught—to always forgive people, no matter how many times they hurt you. It doesn't sound very easy, but I'm really going to try.

Father heard that Jesus was really tired after he fed the crowd of five thousand people. All he wanted to do was to be alone and spend some time in the mountains in prayer with his Father. He knew that his disciples were tired, too. So he said to Peter, "Why don't you and the other disciples row your boat over to Bethsaida? I'll send the crowd away." Then Jesus waved to the disciples, telling them, "Wait for me on the other side of the lake."

> **Remember**
>
> Jesus is inviting me to step out in faith and trust in him.

Out on the lake Peter and the disciples were relaxed and happy. It was good to be away from the crowds. They took turns rowing and talked about the amazing miracle that Jesus had performed that day. How they loved being Jesus' special friends! But the peaceful trip across the lake was about to end. The gentle evening breeze was replaced by a very strong wind. Soon their boat was being tossed about in the rough sea. "Row harder," ordered Peter. Andrew and Philip shouted back, "We're doing our best. But we are heading right into the wind." James yelled, "We are being pushed backward," and John asked, "What are we going to do?" "We must trust God," said Peter.

Suddenly James pointed at a figure that appeared to be walking toward them on the water. "What's that?" he asked in disbelief. "Oh, no, it's a ghost!" another disciple cried. As they clung to each other, the disciples heard a familiar voice. "Take heart. It is I. Don't be afraid." Do you know who it was? Yes! It was Jesus!

But Peter had a hard time believing that it was Jesus walking on the high waves. "Lord," said Peter, "if it is really you, tell me to come to you across the waves." "Come," said Jesus. Helped by Andrew and James, Peter stood up and stepped out of the boat onto the water. He looked right into Jesus' eyes and took one step and then another toward him. He couldn't believe it! He was walking on the water, too! But as soon as Peter took his eyes off Jesus and thought about what he was actually doing, he got very fearful. He looked down at his feet. "Oh no! I'm sinking," shouted Peter. "Help me, Jesus!"

> **Scripture Memory Verse**
>
> "Take heart, it is I; do not be afraid."
> (Matthew 14:27)

Quickly Jesus put out his hand and grabbed Peter. Jesus said, "Peter why did you doubt that you could walk on the water toward me? Your faith is very weak." Then together they walked on the water toward the boat. James, John, and Andrew helped them climb in over the side. Almost immediately, the wind stopped and the sea became very calm. The moon shone brightly, and hundreds of stars twinkled in the sky. Peter, Andrew, James, and John weren't afraid anymore. Together they said, "Jesus, you are truly the Son of God."

Jesus, Speak to Me

Peter stepped out in faith when he got out of the boat and started walking toward me on the water. It's not always easy to trust me, especially when life is "stormy." Is there something in your life right now that you are having a hard time trusting me with? Please tell me about it. Take my hand, and I will help you.

There will be times when I will call you to step out in faith, too. I might want you to talk to someone about me. That might make you uncomfortable or afraid. Or, I might ask you to say no to your friends if they want you to do something that is wrong. That will take courage. Just remember my words and trust in me. Whenever I call you to step out in faith, keep your eyes focused on me. I will always help you!

Prayer

Jesus, I place all my trust in you. Holy Spirit, help me to keep my eyes focused on Jesus at all times.

The Woman Caught in Sin

(John 8:1–11)

It's Mary from Nazareth again. I don't think I've told you about my friend Ned. He's our family donkey. Some people don't think that donkeys are very special. But Ned is!

Do you remember the story of Balaam's talking donkey? Well, Ned has never spoken to me. But I know he likes me. When I pet him or talk to him, he brays. Ned and I have a lot of fun together. When our chores for the day are finished, I sometimes jump on his back and go for a ride over the hills around our house. In some places it is very stony. Ned is very surefooted and never slips. He doesn't walk very fast, but that's okay with me.

Some people take long journeys on donkeys. Whether you are poor or rich, donkeys are the way you travel—unless you are crossing a desert, and then you ride a camel! I've never seen the Sea of Galilee. I'd love to go there one day with Ned. But it is about fifteen miles away, and it would take more than a day to get there. Mary and Joseph took a long journey on a donkey, all the way from Nazareth to Bethlehem just before Jesus was born. Grandmother also told me that Jesus rode a donkey into Jerusalem just before he died. So donkeys are really very special. At least I think so!

> **Remember**
>
> Jesus doesn't want me to judge or criticize other people.

I'm sure you know that Jesus traveled from one town to another either by walking or by boat. But did you know that one of Jesus' favorite places to walk was to the Mount of Olives? This small mountain range just outside of Jerusalem is about two miles long and two hundred feet above the city and is covered with olive groves. Some of the olive trees are really old. Often, at sunset, Jesus would go to a garden on the mount and spend hours talking to his heavenly Father. After praying one night, Jesus taught his disciples to pray the Our Father. Other times, Jesus would walk over the mount on his way to Bethany to visit his friends Mary, Martha, and Lazarus.

From the Mount of Olives, Jesus could walk down to the Temple in Jerusalem. That brings me to the story for today. My grandmother told it to me!

Jesus had been praying all night in his special garden on the Mount of Olives. As the sun began to rise, he knew it was time to share with the people more about God's plan for their lives. As he walked down the paths toward the Temple, people recognized who he was. They said to each other, "Look, there's the Teacher. Let's follow him." Some of them asked, "But how can this man be so clever? He didn't even go to school."

When Jesus got to the Temple, he sat down on a stone in one of the courtyards. Everyone was just gathering around him, when some of the Pharisees and scribes came in with a woman and said, "Make way. Make way. We want to ask Jesus a question." The young woman looked very frightened. One of the elders said, "Jesus, this woman was caught doing something very bad. Do you think we should stone her?" Under the Law of Moses, someone committing such a crime should be stoned, but only our Roman rulers, not the scribes and Pharisees, could put a man or woman to death. However, the Pharisees were trying to test Jesus to see what he would tell them.

Scripture Memory Verse

"I came not to judge the world, but to save the world."

(John 12:47)

Jesus didn't reply to their question. Instead, he bent down and started writing in the sand. They kept questioning him, so finally he straightened up and said, "The person who has never done anything wrong can throw the first stone." Then he bent down again to write in the sand. Everyone became very quiet. They didn't know what to say! One by one, all the elders walked away.

When the last elder had gone, Jesus looked up and said, "Woman, where has everyone gone? Did no one throw a stone at you?" "No one, sir," she replied. Jesus looked kindly at the woman and said, "I want you to leave here. Go back to your home. But from now on, do not sin. Try to live a life that is pleasing to God." With a big smile on her face, the woman said, "Oh Jesus, thank you. I will do what is right!"

Can you guess what the woman did next? She went home and told her family and friends all about Jesus and how wonderful he was. How merciful Jesus was to the woman!

Jesus, Speak to Me

Do you know what I was thinking about the woman that the Pharisees brought to me? I knew that she was not living a life pleasing to God. But I didn't come to judge her. I loved her. I wanted her to be holy. Her life really changed after we met. She knew that I loved her, and my love gave her the courage to keep my commandments.

Sometimes people can be judgmental and think of themselves as superior to others. Do you judge people you know? Perhaps you are tempted to judge your friends based on what they wear, what music they listen to, or what they do or don't do. Think about other ways that people judge each other. How can you be more loving? During Lent, watch out for those judgmental thoughts!

Prayer

Holy Spirit, please help me to stop judging people. I want to love as Jesus loved.

A Family Journey with Jesus through Lent
Fifth Week
of Lent

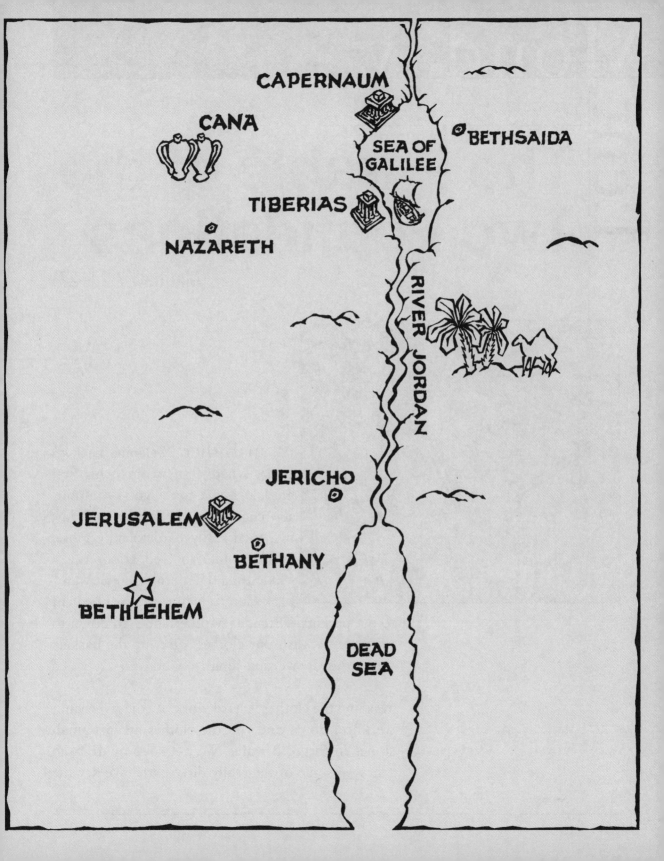

week 5 | day 1

The Parable of the Two Foundations

(Matthew 7:24–27)

I'm Esther. Welcome back to Cana, where Jesus worked his first miracle. I have to tell you—that miracle changed my life. Since that day, I've tried really hard to pray more. I usually talk to God as soon as I wake up in the mornings. Every day, I ask God to help me to be obedient to my parents. Often, as Mother and I go down to the river to wash our clothes, carrying the baskets on our heads, we sing songs to God.

Washing the clothes is hard work. At the riverbank, we kneel down and rub the clothes against small stones in the cold water. We put soap made from ashes on some of the really dirty parts. We dry the clothes by spreading them out on the rocks. After we're finished, I love to dangle my feet in the cool, sparkling water!

Just last week I met my friend Joanna at the river. While we were waiting for our clothes to dry in the hot midday sun, she told me that her heart had also been changed. She had just returned from visiting her aunt in Capernaum. There she had heard Jesus teach.

According to Joanna, Jesus had said, "We must not try to get back at someone who has upset us or hurt us. We must pray for that person." Jesus also said: "Be generous with your time and money. If people have a need, help them—even those you don't like very much. Treat other people as you would like to be treated." Then Joanna told me one of Jesus' parables.

> ## Remember
>
> Jesus wants me to make good choices. I will make good choices when the foundation of my life is prayer, Scripture, and what my parents and the Church teach me.

Two men were talking one day about building new homes. Nathan, the first man, sat down and thought a long time about where and how to build his house. He wanted to find a good place to build the house, where he could lay the foundation on rock. When he had found just the right spot, he dug deep into the solid ground and began to build. It was a lot of work, but finally the house was finished! "I've done a good job," said Nathan. "This is a solid house." His wife and children were very happy. That night they slept in their new home.

While they were all sleeping, a strong wind began to blow, thunder crashed, lightning flashed, and rain came down in buckets! They all woke up, very frightened. But Nathan said, "Don't worry." He was right! Because Nathan had built the house on rock, it didn't get blown over in the wind. Nathan's family didn't get wet.

Now at the same time, the other man, Zadok, started to build his house. But he was in a hurry. "I'll just go out and find a piece of land and start building my house," he said to himself. So he went to the river. There the soil was very sandy and easy to dig. "I'll just build my house here," he said. He finished the house quickly. His wife and children moved in. They were also very happy in their house.

Scripture Memory Verse

"Everyone then who hears these words of mine and acts on them will be like a wise man who built his house on rock." (Matthew 7:24)

Can you guess what happened on the day of the violent storm? While Nathan was safe inside his house, Zadok was in terrible trouble. The wind shook the house, and some of the walls started to fall in. The roof was blown off, and the rain poured in. Zadok's wife was not very happy anymore! When they looked out the door, their house was in a deep puddle of water. Finally the whole house collapsed. Zadok and his family managed to escape, and they climbed into some nearby trees. They cried as they saw their new house being swept away in the river.

"Joanna, why did Jesus tell this parable?" I asked. She explained, "Jesus wants us to base our lives on him. Then when we find ourselves in difficult times, we will not be shaken. It's hard work to build our lives on Jesus, but it's worth it!"

Jesus, Speak to Me

Good choices, bad choices! The second man paid a terrible price for choosing to build his house on a sandy foundation, didn't he? What do you think he did the next time he built a house?

How many choices do you think you make every day? What happens every time you have to make a choice? Do you take the time to think about it first?

Many choices have consequences, so it's important to think first before you act. Your brother or sister might annoy you today. What will you do? Will you say something mean, or will you try to ignore what is annoying you? Maybe you are taking a test, and you can see the answers to the problems on your classmate's paper. Will you look at the answers, or turn your head away? It's your choice!

Prayer

Jesus, I choose you to be the foundation of my life. Holy Spirit, give me the desire to pray and read Scripture every day.

You have a great foundation—your faith in me. So remember that your house is built on solid rock! Think about the choices you have before you do something wrong. I have given you the gift of free will, which means that you can choose to follow me or not. How about telling someone right now about a good choice you made today?

Jesus Raises Lazarus from the Dead

(John 11:1–44)

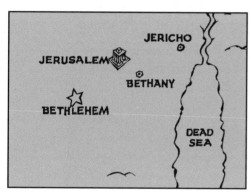

You are back in Bethany with me, Reuben. I love living here because we are so near Jerusalem. My aunt lives there, and quite often Mother will ask Rachel and me, "Would you like to go to visit your cousins today in Jerusalem?" Our answer is always, "Yes!" We often bring some treats to them—some of Mother's delicious raisin barley cakes and fresh figs, together with honey that Mother buys in the market, and even some popped corn.

We were just about to leave on one of our visits to Jerusalem when Martha, my mother's friend, came rushing to the door, almost in tears. "What's happened?" asked Mother. "My brother, Lazarus, woke up early this morning feeling very sick. Mary and I are so worried about him," said Martha. She told us that Lazarus had never been so sick before.

"Is there anything we can do?" asked Mother. "Could Reuben get a message to Jesus?" Martha asked. Everyone knew that Jesus would be able to heal Lazarus. "Yes, I can!" I said.

Off I ran, as fast as I could. I wasn't interested in anything except getting the news to Jesus. I found one of his followers, who knew that he was preaching in the villages to the North. "Can you come with me to find Jesus, so I can tell him that his friend Lazarus is sick?" I asked. "His sisters are worried that he will die unless Jesus comes and heals him." The disciple hurried off with me. Finally, a day later, we found Jesus. But he said, "Lazarus will not die. His sickness will show everyone how great God is."

> **Remember**
>
> Jesus gave me new life at baptism!

I waited for Jesus to say, "I'm off to Bethany." But Jesus didn't go that day. He didn't go the next day, either. The following day, I heard Jesus say to his disciples, "Now it's time for me to go to Lazarus." Some of the disciples were worried and said, "Jesus, the people there want to kill you. Don't go back." But Jesus said, "I must go. Lazarus is dead."

As Jesus went down the path toward Bethany, Martha saw him. She rushed out to meet him. With tears streaming down her face, she sobbed, "Jesus, Lazarus is dead. We buried him four days ago. If you had been here, he wouldn't have died." Jesus put his arm around Martha and said, "Trust me. Your brother will live again." "I know," said Martha. "He will live forever in heaven."

All this time, Lazarus' sister Mary was inside the house crying. Many of their friends were there, and they were also weeping. Others were playing sad music on the reed pipes. But when someone told Mary that Jesus was coming down the path, she ran to meet him. Falling down at his feet she cried out, "Jesus, if you had been here, my brother would still be alive." Jesus asked, "Mary, where have you put Lazarus' body?" "In a cave cut into the hillside," Mary replied. So they

Scripture Memory Verse

"I am the resurrection and the life. Those who believe in me, even though they die, will live."

(John 11:25)

led Jesus to the cave, which had a stone covering the opening. Jesus stood there and cried.

Then Jesus said, "Roll the stone away." Martha was surprised and said, "Jesus, Lazarus has been dead for four days." Jesus replied, "Didn't I tell you, Martha, that if you believe in me you will see how great God is?" As the stone was being rolled away from the opening, Jesus looked up to heaven and prayed to his Father. In a loud voice, Jesus said, "Lazarus, come out!" At first nothing happened. But then someone near the opening to the cave shouted, "Look! I can see something white in the darkness. It must be Lazarus." After a few moments, Lazarus stood in the daylight. His face, arms, and legs were wrapped in strips of white cloth. "Take off his burial clothes so that he can see and walk," said Jesus.

I watched as Mary and Martha hugged Lazarus. I heard them say, "Jesus, thank you for giving Lazarus a new life!" Lazarus was alive! Jesus had raised his friend from the dead.

Jesus, Speak to Me

I gave Lazarus a new life when I called him out of the tomb! The day that you were baptized, I gave you a new life. What does that mean? It means that the Holy Spirit dwells in you. It means that you are part of my family—you are my brothers and sisters, and we have the same Father! It means that I will give you the grace to live a life for my glory—a life that will show others that I am real and that my love is forever. What a blessing new life is!

Just as you keep your natural life healthy by eating, sleeping, and exercising, so you can keep your spiritual life healthy by praying, reading the Scriptures, and regularly receiving the sacraments. All these things make the new life I gave you at baptism continue to grow.

When Lazarus came out of the tomb, his whole body was covered with binding cloths. After they were taken off, he could live his new life. Lent is a good time to take off any "binding cloths" that are stopping you from living your new life to the fullest. A binding cloth could be jealousy, selfishness, or anger. Can you think of any others?

Prayer

Father, I want the new life that you gave me at baptism to grow. Holy Spirit, remove the binding cloths that prevent me in any way from living this new life.

week 5 | day 3

Jesus Heals the Centurion's Servant

(Luke 7:1–10)

Hello again! I'm Jacob from Capernaum. Since I last told you a story, I've learned how to fish with a spear! I'm very proud of myself. Father taught me late one afternoon, after he had finished mending some of his nets. The lake was smooth, and the sky was cloudless, so we could tell that there was no chance of a storm. Remember, the storms on the lake can be very, very dangerous. So we got into his boat and rowed just a little way off from the shore. "Now, get your spear ready," said Father. "When a fish swims near the surface of the water, spear it." As you might guess, that was easier said than done! I missed so many times!

But I kept on trying. Just as the sun was setting, I speared my first fish. "Look Father, I've got one!" After that, I speared three more. I knew that Mother would be happy to have fish for dinner the next day.

I had so much fun with my dad that evening. On the way home, we laughed and joked. He also told me a story that he had heard at the lake that day. It was about a Roman centurion. Centurions are Roman officers who are in charge of a hundred soldiers. Well, I want to tell you about a miracle Jesus performed for a centurion right here in Capernaum. This centurion was very popular because he was such a generous man. He had even paid for the building of our synagogue with his own money.

One day the centurion's favorite servant became very ill. He was worried and thought to himself, "I don't want my servant to die. What can I do?" Then he remembered hearing about a man named Jesus, who healed sick people. He called in some of the Jewish elders and said, "Please go and find Jesus and ask him to come and heal my servant."

Jesus was just coming into Capernaum when the elders found him. "Jesus, the servant of a Roman centurion is very sick. The centurion is a very good man who loves our country and built our synagogue. Please come to his house and heal his servant." "I'd be happy to come with you," replied Jesus.

> **Remember**
>
> I can have faith like the centurion's and believe in Jesus' power even though I can't see him.

So Jesus, the elders, and some of the disciples walked quickly along the streets leading to the centurion's house. They had almost reached the house when they were stopped by some of the centurion's friends. "Jesus, we have a message for you. This is what the centurion wants to say to you: 'Jesus, please don't take up your time by coming to my house. I'm not good enough for you to visit me. I didn't come to you myself, because I'm not good enough to meet you.'"

"Did the centurion say anything else?" asked Jesus. "Yes," said one of the friends. "This is the rest of the message: 'Jesus, I know that if you just say the word, my servant will be healed. I have a hundred soldiers under me, and if I tell them to do something, they will do it. So I know that your words have power.'"

> ### Scripture Memory Verse
>
> "Lord, I am not worthy to receive you. Only say the word and I shall be healed."
>
> (Adapted for Mass from Luke 7:7)

Jesus was so amazed at this message. He turned to everyone standing around him and said, "This centurion really loves and trusts God!"

This story has a great ending. When the friends got back to the centurion's house, the servant ran out to meet them, shouting, "I'm healed! I'm healed!" Standing at the doorway was the centurion, smiling and praising God.

Jesus, Speak to Me

What really pleased me about the centurion was that he trusted that I could help him. So when his servant got sick, he sent for me. He didn't even have to see me in person. He knew that my word had power, and that I could heal his servant, even if I didn't go to his home.

I want you to have faith in my power, just like the centurion did. My word still has power today, even though I no longer walk the earth. You don't have to see me in person to know that I will hear your prayers. I can act today in the world just as I did two thousand years ago. I still live among you!

Can you think of a time when you saw my power at work, either in your life or in the life of someone you know? It's good to remember these stories. The centurion had faith in me because he had heard the stories about my miracles. It will help you build up your faith when you share stories about me and how I respond to the prayers of my people. Can you share a modern-day story about me right now? How about writing one down in your journal?

Prayer

Jesus, you are alive in the world today. Give me the eyes of faith to see your power and glory.

The Parable of the Good Samaritan

(Luke 10:25–37)

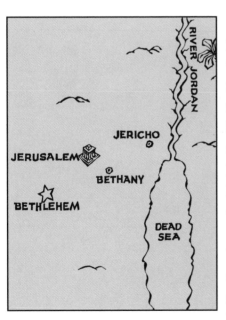

Benjamin from Jerusalem here! Do you know that it's almost time for Passover? I can't wait! Passover is when we remember how God miraculously helped Moses and our people escape from slavery in Egypt. Pharaoh, the king of Egypt, had refused to let the Hebrew people leave his country. So God sent an angel of death to take all of Egypt's firstborn sons. The angel "passed over" the homes of the Hebrews where the blood of a lamb was painted on the door.

When we celebrate Passover, the high priest offers the sacrifice of a lamb. Every family has a special meal together. In addition to roasted lamb, we eat bitter herbs, to remind us of all those bitter years of slavery, and unleavened bread, because the Hebrews had to leave in such a hurry that they didn't have time to let the bread rise. During the meal, the youngest son asks his father questions about the night of the exodus from Egypt.

Speaking of questions, I want to tell you about a question someone asked Jesus. My father heard about it in one of the Temple courtyards.

I should tell you first that the Pharisees didn't always like Jesus' teachings, so sometimes they tried to trick him. One day, one of the experts in the law asked, "Jesus, how can I please God and go to heaven when I die?" Jesus replied, "That's a very good question. What you need to do is to love God and love your neighbor." Then the lawyer asked, "And who is my neighbor?" Jesus then said, "I'll tell you a story that I hope will answer your question:

> **Remember**
>
> Be on the lookout for those in need, and take the time to help them.

"Early one morning, a man left Jerusalem on a journey to Jericho. He wore his newest tunic, cloak, and sandals. Two money bags hung on the leather belt around his waist. After walking over some hills, the man saw a stream. 'Oh, I can't wait for a cool drink of water,' he said to himself. He started off down the rocky, dusty path to the stream. There was no one else around—or so he thought.

"Suddenly, four robbers jumped out from behind a rock. They knocked him to the ground, and beat him so badly that he couldn't move. Then they took his bags of money and his new clothes and ran away.

"The injured man lay in the hot sun for a long time. All he could do was pray that someone would come along this lonely road to help him. Finally he heard footsteps. He looked up and saw a priest from the Temple in his fine clothes coming toward him. 'Great! This priest will help me,' he thought. But guess what? The priest was busy reading his prayers and didn't stop to help him.

"Some time later the man heard someone singing praises to God. 'What beautiful singing. That must be a Levite from the Temple. I'm sure he'll stop and help me,' the man thought. He tried to call for help, but he was too weak to speak. Did the Levite see the injured man? Yes! But he pretended that he didn't, and he walked over to the other side of the road.

Scripture Memory Verse

"Truly I tell you, just as you did it to one of the least of these who are members of my family, you did it to me."

(Matthew 25:40)

"'Won't anyone help me?' cried the man. Suddenly along the path came a stranger riding on a donkey. 'Oh no, it's a Samaritan. He won't help me. He's one of our enemies,' the man thought to himself. So he was really surprised when the Samaritan came over to him and said, 'It looks like you need help.' The Samaritan got off his donkey. Very gently, he cleansed and soothed the injured man's wounds with wine and olive oil, and then wrapped his cuts and bruises in bandages. Then he gave the man a long, cool drink from his water flask.

"'I can't leave you here,' said the Samaritan. 'I'm going to put you on my donkey and take you to an inn in Jericho.' When they got to the inn, the Samaritan said to the owner, 'This man has been attacked by robbers. He's injured. Here's money for him to stay in one of your rooms until he's better. If that's not enough, I'll give you more when I return.'"

After Jesus had finished the story, he asked, "Which of those three men was a good neighbor to the man who was injured?" The lawyer replied, "The one who stopped and helped the man." Jesus looked at the lawyer and said, "You're right. Now go off and be a good neighbor, too."

Jesus, Speak to Me

Prayer

Jesus, I want to be like the Good Samaritan. Help me to be aware of the needs of others.

The priest and the Levite were so wrapped up in their own worlds that they didn't stop to help the injured man. Like them, sometimes you can be so wrapped up in yourself and your own concerns that you are not aware of someone else's need. Or, you may feel too busy to help or be afraid of getting involved. The Good Samaritan was happy to help, even though it cost him time and money. It often costs us something to help others in need—usually time, money, or both. But when you help others, you are really helping me in the work of building my kingdom!

Lent is a great time to think about how you can be a Good Samaritan. Pray for a generous heart. If there is a child at school or in your neighborhood who is lonely, perhaps you could befriend him. If you have a friend or a relative who is sick, stop in for a visit or give her a phone call. Help your brothers and sisters with their chores around the house, even if they don't ask you. Remember, people will know you are my followers by your love for one another!

A Paralytic Is Carried by Friends

(Luke 5:17–26)

Hello! It's Joshua from Bethsaida. It's harvest time here right now. This morning my father asked me to go with him to some fields that belong to a wealthy farmer. The farmer was waiting for us. He looked very happy to see me. "Joshua, you will be a big help today in harvesting the wheat," he said.

Father and the men cut the stalks of wheat with a wooden sickle, which had sharp flints set into the cutting edge. My job was to pick up the wheat and carry it to a threshing floor. This is where it would be ground into grain with a big stone that two oxen turn by walking around in circles. Later that day, with a long-pronged fork, we tossed the wheat up in the air. The wind blew the light straw away from the floor, and the grain fell to the ground. Some of the boys working there bundled up the straw, while others put the grain into large bags.

As the sun set, Father and I reached our home. I was exhausted! "Good day's work, Joshua," said Father. "Now I'm going to tell you about some other men who worked really hard!" Here's the story my father told me:

In Capernaum there was a man called Amos, who couldn't walk. The only way he could get around his small house was to drag his body across the floor. He had a kind wife and two sons, who took good care of him. Amos also had four special friends who came to visit him every day. Amos and his friends would sit and talk for hours.

> **Remember**
>
> A good friend can bring others to Jesus.

One day, Amos' friends arrived with some great news. "Amos, Jesus is back in town!" they exclaimed. "Oh, please take me to see Jesus. I know he can heal me," Amos said. Amos' wife was really excited. "I've heard that he's already healed people who can't walk and those who are blind and deaf. He has even set free those who had demons." "Let's take Amos to see Jesus," said the friends, as his wife ran off to find Amos' bed mat.

Amos' friends knew exactly where to go. They had heard that Jesus was at Peter's house. But what they didn't know was that the Pharisees and people from all over Galilee had come to listen to Jesus, too. Many brought their loved ones to be healed. There were people everywhere!

"Oh, no!" cried Amos. "I'm never going to be healed. Jesus won't be able to see me." "Don't worry," said one of his friends. "Let's think! How can we get you to Jesus? We're not going to give up yet."

Then they had a great idea. Around the back of Peter's house was the stairway leading to the roof. Amos' friends carried him up the stairs and over the little wall and laid him down on the roof. They started to take off bits of straw and mud tiles from the roof. "What are you doing?" asked Amos. "You just wait and see!" whispered one of his friends.

After about ten minutes, Amos' friends had made a hole in the roof. Then each friend took a corner of Amos' mat. "What are you doing?" Amos asked, rather nervously. "Don't worry!" they replied. Very carefully they held Amos' mat over the hole in the roof and lowered him down.

> **Scripture Memory Verse**
>
> "Faithful friends are a sturdy shelter: whoever finds one has found a treasure."
>
> (Sirach 6:14)

"What's happening?" asked one of the Pharisees. Peter's wife said, "A man is coming through my roof!" Then Amos heard a very kind voice. "Put the man down here. Gently, gently!" Amos knew it was Jesus. "Oh Jesus, can you heal me?" said Amos with tears in his eyes. "Friend, your sins are forgiven." This made the scribes and Pharisees angry. They said, "Only God can forgive sins!"

Jesus replied, "Which is easier—to say, 'your sins are forgiven you' or to say, 'stand up and walk'?" Then he turned to Amos. "So that everyone knows that I can forgive sins, I say to you, stand up, pick up your mat, and go home." Amos jumped to his feet, shouting, "Praise God! I'm healed. Jesus has healed me." He waved to his friends, who were leaning over the hole in the roof, and yelled up to them, "Thank you so much for bringing me to Jesus. You are great friends!" Others exclaimed, "We have seen great things today."

Jesus, Speak to Me

A good friend is a special gift. I'll bet you enjoy your friends, and they enjoy you. Amos certainly was grateful for his four friends. I want you to be a good and loving friend. Here's a quiz about friendship. Give yourself a point for each time you answer yes.

- *Good friends are reliable.* Do your friends know that if you say you will do something, you will really do it?
- *Good friends are faithful.* Do your friends know that you will work through differences with them and not say, "I'm not your friend anymore," when something goes wrong?
- *Good friends are loyal.* Do your friends know that you won't gossip about them behind their backs?
- *Good friends follow God's teachings.* Do your friends look up to you and know that you will only do what is right and pleasing to Jesus and your parents?
- *Good friends are helpful.* Do your friends know that you will help them when they have a special need and won't say, "I'm too busy"?

What was your score? If you need to make some changes, Lent is a great time to start!

> **Prayer**
>
> Father, thank you for all my friends. Holy Spirit, help me to be a good friend to others.

The Parable of the Wedding Banquet

(Matthew: 22:1–14)

I'm Hannah from Tiberias, and I have a question for you. Have you ever read the story about Hannah, the mother of Samuel? It's a great story about a woman of faith. Hannah really wanted a child. She promised God that if she had a son, she would make sure that he served God. My mother says that one of the ways I can serve God is by doing the right thing, like "turning the other cheek" with my sister and brother when they irritate me. It's not always easy, but when I try to please God, I feel really happy inside.

Talking about being happy, another kind of happiness is when I go out first thing in the morning to find the eggs that our six chickens have laid! They are so lovely and warm when I pick them up out of the straw. I handle them very gently so that I won't break the shells. But last week I tripped over a stone and broke three of them. Mother wasn't angry with me, because she knew it was an accident. When I told her, she said, "What a great excuse to make a special lentil loaf for dinner!"

That brings me to the parable Jesus told during dinner one Sabbath at the home of a Pharisee. Jesus wanted to talk about heaven, so he compared it to a wedding feast. Guess where I heard this parable? Down at the well!

There was a king who had a son he loved very much. One day the son came to the father and said, "Father, I want to get married." Oh, the king was so happy. Together they talked about all the special guests who were to be invited.

> **Remember**
>
> My Father longs to fill me with his heavenly food at Mass.

After weeks of preparation, the wedding day arrived. When the ceremony had ended, the king instructed his servants to announce to the specially invited guests that the wedding feast was about to begin!

But on the first day, not one of the specially invited guests arrived. The king was so disappointed. Then he thought, "Surely they will come tomorrow." So the next day he sent the servants out again to announce to them that the wedding feast had begun. "Tell them I have prepared the best and most expensive foods," said the king. All day he looked out the doorway, hoping to see some guests walking toward the house. He waited and waited. As the sun was setting, he saw his servants coming back. "Where are the guests that I invited to my son's wedding feast?" asked the king. "They wouldn't come," said one of the servants. "What do you mean, they wouldn't come? What excuses did they give you?" asked the king, who was now very angry.

The first servant said, "My guest said he has just bought a new team of oxen and wants to plow his fields."

> **Scripture Memory Verse**
>
> "Many are called, but few are chosen."
> (Matthew 22:14)

The second servant said, "My guest said that he has just purchased a new piece of land, and wants to look at it again to plan what crops he will grow."

The third servant said, "My guest said that he has just gotten married and wants to spend time alone with his new wife."

"So those are the excuses!" said the king. He thought for a moment. Then he said to his servants, "I have an idea! Go out into the countryside and invite anyone who wants to come—whether they are good or bad! Let them enjoy the food, wine, singing, and dancing at my son's wedding feast. Go quickly."

Newly invited guests came from everywhere! The king was so pleased. His kingdom hall was full. The king said, "Many are called, but few are chosen."

Jesus, Speak to Me

When you were baptized, you received a special invitation to a wedding banquet. In heaven, there's a banquet going on all the time. Here on earth, there's also a wedding banquet—the Mass, which is offered in Catholic parishes all over the world every single day. What a wonderful celebration! I want you to come as often as you can!

I call everyone to this celebration, but many choose not to come. They often have excuses for not coming. Here are a few common ones: "I'm too busy"; "I want to watch TV"; or "I don't feel like it today." If you are tempted to use one of those excuses, remember the parable about the king. How hurt you would be if you threw a big party and no one came!

Prayer

Father, thank you for inviting me to your wedding feast, the Mass. I love to receive the heavenly food of your Son, Jesus.

A Family Journey with Jesus through Lent

Sixth Week
of Lent

Jesus' Entry into Jerusalem

(Matthew 21:1–10; Luke 19:28–44)

It's Judith from Jerusalem. I hope you've enjoyed the stories you've heard so far about the life of Jesus. Over the next two weeks, Jesus' disciples are going to tell you what happened in the days leading up to his arrest and death on the cross. So please stay with us.

Here's what happened the day the crowd gave Jesus a great welcome as he rode into Jerusalem. Thomas, one of Jesus' disciples, told a group of us about it after Jesus' resurrection. This is what he said:

"Jesus really wanted to be in Jerusalem for the feast of the Passover, but only he knew that it was going to be the last one he would celebrate with us. As we were walking over the Mount of Olives near Bethphage, Jesus said to two of the disciples, 'Do you see that town over there? Go there, and as you enter it, you will see a donkey with its colt. Untie the colt and bring it to me. If anyone asks you what you are doing, tell them that the Master needs it.'

"The two disciples were puzzled, but they did what Jesus asked. I watched them until they were out of sight. Then I asked Jesus, 'Will they find the donkey and her colt?' Jesus didn't answer, but after a short time, I saw them coming back with a colt. It was so young that no one had ever ridden it before. There was no time to find a saddle, so we put some of our cloaks on its back. After petting the colt, Jesus got on its back and rode toward Jerusalem.

> **Remember**
>
> Praising God helps you remember how much you love God and how much he loves you.

"Then a beautiful thing happened. A group of people had been following Jesus since they spotted him coming down the Mount of Olives. As Jesus began to ride toward Jerusalem, they started cheering, 'Jesus, we love you. Jesus, we thank you for healing us. Jesus, we thank you for teaching us about God's love.' Children were waving palm branches in the air, laughing and singing, 'Jesus is going to Jerusalem. Jesus is going to Jerusalem, riding on a colt!'

"The crowd grew bigger and bigger. Many men and women, young and old, ran ahead of Jesus to pick palm leaves. They laid these on the ground for the colt to walk over. Others took off their cloaks and put them down. Jesus was riding the colt over a beautiful carpet! He looked just like a king, except that he was riding on a donkey, a poor man's animal. I thought to myself, 'Jesus is truly humble.'

"Singing filled the air: 'Hosanna to the Son of David! Blessed is he who comes in the name of the Lord! Hosanna in the highest.' Others shouted out, 'This is Jesus, the prophet from Nazareth in Galilee.' I thought it was wonderful. But some of the Pharisees who were watching went over to Jesus and said, 'Teacher, tell your followers to stop singing your praises.' Jesus looked at them and said, 'If they keep quiet, the stones will cry out!'

> **Scripture Memory Verse**
>
> "Praise the LORD! Praise the LORD from the heavens; praise him in the heights!"
> (Psalm 148:1)

"As Jesus rode along, the Temple in Jerusalem came into view. How Jesus loved the great city of Jerusalem. Suddenly he stopped. I saw him begin to cry. I didn't know why, but perhaps Jesus knew that something sad was going to happen in Jerusalem in the future.

"Jesus' sadness didn't last too long. As soon as he turned to look again at the crowd, he began to smile."

Jesus, Speak to Me

On the night I was born, the angels praised and worshipped my Father, singing, "Glory to God in the highest." Right now there are tens of thousands of angels in heaven singing praises to my Father! They are singing, "Amen! Praise and glory to our God forever and ever!"

Why do you think it's important to praise my Father? He doesn't need it—he's already so great and awesome. But praise helps *you*! It's a way you can express your love for your heavenly Father and for me. If you are feeling sad, praising God will make you feel happy, because you will remember how much my Father and I love you. Whenever you praise and sing songs, you are joining with the angels before my throne!

Sing to me often. Make up your own song—of praise for who I am, and of thanksgiving for all that I have done for you and your family. It makes me so happy to hear you! Sing along to a CD at home or in the car. Don't miss a day of singing my praises—the angels don't!

Prayer

Father, Son, and Holy Spirit, I love you, praise you, and worship you!

Jesus Drives the Traders Out of the Temple

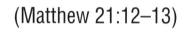

(Matthew 21:12–13)

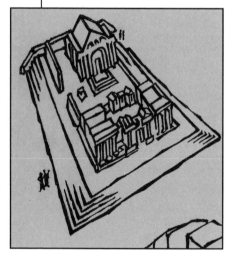

Judith from Jerusalem, here again. Today the apostle Thomas is going to continue telling you about the day that Jesus went to Jerusalem for the Feast of the Passover. He remembers the day very well:

"On the way to Jerusalem, Jesus said several times, 'I love going to the Temple in Jerusalem to worship with my Father's children.' I had been with him for three years now, and Jesus was always talking to us about his relationship with his Father in heaven. I will always remember when Jesus said, 'The Father and I are one.'

"The crowds waving palm branches followed Jesus all the way from the Mount of Olives to the city gate. So many people had heard that Jesus of Nazareth was coming to the city. They wanted to know, 'Who is this man?' Eventually, however, the crowds thinned out. Jesus set off to the Temple so that he could pray, and we disciples accompanied him.

> **Remember**
>
> I will treat my body with respect because I am a temple of the Holy Spirit.

"As we were walking by the Temple walls into the courtyard, we heard loud voices. Jesus looked at us and asked, 'What's all the noise? That's not the singing of praises to God.' As we entered the courtyard, he gasped, 'What's happening here?'

"Jesus was shocked to see that the traders had moved their tables from outside the Temple walls into the courtyard, a place of prayer. People wanting to buy sacrifices for the Passover were rushing from one table to another, looking at the caged birds. Others were inspecting the sheep, lambs, and goats tied to the legs of tables. The noise and smells were terrible. There were moneychangers with their scales sitting in every corner. They told the passersby that they had the best rate of exchange of regular money for the Temple coin—the shekel. Anyone wanting to buy anything had to pay with a shekel. Everyone knew that some moneychangers were not honest and often kept too much of the money for themselves when they made their exchanges.

> **Scripture Memory Verse**
>
> "Do you not know that your body is a temple of the Holy Spirit within you?"
> (1 Corinthians 6:19)

"Jesus was angrier than I have ever seen him. He shouted at the traders, 'This is a holy place—a place of prayer. It's my Father's house. You have made it a den of thieves!' Then Jesus started turning over some of the tables. Birds escaped from their cages. Animals broke loose from their tethers. Coins spilled all over the ground. Many of the traders knew that they had done wrong. They quickly picked up their tables, chairs, money bags, and animals and left the courtyard. Others were not so quick to leave. But Jesus would not let anyone stay. 'This is my Father's house. It is a place of prayer,' Jesus said over and over again.

"Just as the last traders left the courtyard, people started to come to Jesus to be healed. He laid his hands on them and performed many miracles that day. The religious leaders were not happy with Jesus, and they began to plan how they could get rid of him."

Jesus, Speak to Me

The Temple was a holy place because that was where my Father was worshiped. Did you know that your body is a temple—a temple of the Holy Spirit? That means that your body is a holy place. When you were baptized, the Holy Spirit came to live in you. Every time you receive me in the Eucharist, I come into your temple. I hope you know that I love coming to you.

Because you are a temple of the Holy Spirit, it's important that you treat your body with respect. What are some ways you can do that? You can care for your body by keeping it clean, by eating healthy foods, and by getting enough exercise and sleep. Drugs and alcohol can hurt both your body and your mind. I want you to respect your body by not using these things.

I just want to say one more thing to you. Everyone who is baptized is a temple of the Holy Spirit. You are surrounded by holy temples! Let that truth be a challenge to you to love and respect everyone you see each day.

Prayer

Holy Spirit, thank you for making your home in me.

Judas' Betrayal

(Matthew 26:14–25)

I'm Samuel. You're back in Jericho, but not for long, because I'm going to tell you a story about Jesus that will take you to Jerusalem again! I heard it from Peter, James, and John—three of Jesus' closest disciples—who were passing through Jericho after Jesus' resurrection. This is what John told us:

"All of us who followed Jesus knew that the religious leaders didn't always understand or agree with him. In fact, many of them wanted to get rid of Jesus—perhaps by handing him over to the Roman authorities. But I didn't think that they would actually kill him.

"One night Judas Iscariot, who was also one of Jesus' disciples, secretly left the rest of us and found the house of Caiaphas, the Temple high priest, who was meeting with some of the religious leaders. Judas told them that if they gave him thirty pieces of silver, he would betray Jesus. After that meeting, Judas was always asking Jesus where he was going and how long he would be there. I didn't think much about it at the time, but looking back, I realize that Judas had to let the chief priests know where they could find Jesus when he was not surrounded by a crowd. Remember, many people loved Jesus, and if they saw that he was being arrested, they might have tried to save him by fighting with the soldiers.

> ## Remember
> Jesus wants me to love him more than anything else.

"A few days before the Passover, we were again in Bethany. Jesus said to Peter and me, 'I would like you two to go to Jerusalem. As you enter the city, you will see a man carrying a water jar. Ask him if your Master can have the Passover meal in the upper room of his house.'

"Off we went. Peter was the first to see the man with the water jar on his head. We walked quickly and caught up with him. 'Excuse me,' we said. 'We have a question. Our Master would like to have the Passover meal in the upper room of your house. Can he do that?' 'Yes!' the man said. 'There is no one using my upper room. I'd be happy for you to use it.' Then he added, 'I will ask my wife and children to help prepare all the special foods you will need for the Passover meal.'

"Peter and I watched—and helped a little, too—as the lamb was roasted, the bitter herbs were washed and chopped, and the sweet *haroset* sauce was made. The house was filled with the smell of lamb roasting and bread baking. It made me so hungry!

"As the sun was setting, Jesus and the other disciples arrived at the upper room. There were thirteen cushions around the low table. I chose one next to

Jesus—I loved being very near him. Jesus said a prayer of thanksgiving, and the feast began. But as we were eating the meal, I thought to myself, 'Jesus looks so sad tonight. I wonder what he's thinking about.'

Scripture Memory Verse

"You cannot serve God and wealth."

(Luke 16:13)

"I soon got my answer. Jesus said, 'Tonight one of you is going to betray me.' I was shocked. Some of us asked, 'Is it I, Jesus?' Others asked, 'Jesus, am I the one?' Jesus was dipping some bitter herbs in the sweet sauce. He stopped and said, 'It is the one who has his hand in the dish along with mine.' I looked. It was Judas. He had a strange look on his face. With tears in his eyes, Jesus said, 'Judas, go and do what you have agreed to do.' I didn't understand what Jesus meant. I thought that perhaps Judas was going to give some money to the poor, because he was in charge of our money.

"We all know now that Judas went to back to Caiaphas and told him that after the Passover meal Jesus might go with his disciples to a garden on the Mount of Olives."

Jesus, Speak to Me

My love for Judas never stopped, even though he betrayed me. But my heart was broken when he decided that money was more important than our friendship.

Have you ever loved something so much that you broke one of my commandments to get it? Perhaps you were so eager to play a video game that you disobeyed your parents and played it when you were supposed to be doing something else. Perhaps you wanted to play with one of your brother's or sister's toys so much that you took it from their room without asking.

Ask my forgiveness now for the times when you put something or someone before me. If you haven't already done so, don't miss the opportunity to go to confession before Easter Sunday. I want to give you the special grace of the Sacrament of Reconciliation.

Prayer

Holy Spirit, help me to be true to Jesus, even when I am tempted to turn away from him.

The Last Supper

(John 13:1–20; Matthew 26:26–30)

Hello! It's Samuel again. I'm so pleased that you have come back to hear more about the last Passover that Jesus celebrated with his disciples. Yesterday you heard all about how Jesus' two disciples, Peter and John, planned the Passover meal and how Judas agreed to betray Jesus. Here's Peter, telling about what happened next that night:

"One thing I've learned from being with Jesus for three years is that I should never be surprised at what he does! He walked on water. He was transfigured right before our eyes. He even raised his friend Lazarus from the dead! Well, I have to admit that I was surprised again that evening.

"We were reclining at the table when Jesus suddenly got up off his cushion and left the table. I watched him go over to the side of the room, where there was a bowl, a jug of water, and a towel. He turned and said, 'I want to answer the question two of you asked about who will get the best place in heaven.' I waited for Jesus to say something, but he didn't. Instead, he took off his outer robe, tucked the towel into his belt, and poured some water into the bowl.

> **Remember**
>
> God calls all of his people to be his servants, and some in a special way.

"'No, Jesus! Don't do that,' I said. Jesus was bending down at my feet and was about to pour water over them. I couldn't believe what he was going to do. Jesus was my teacher and my friend. I knew in my heart that he was the Son of God. Washing feet was a servant's job. Servants would meet guests at the door of their master's house with a special footbath, soaking their feet in the cool water to get off all the dust and dirt and then drying them with a clean towel. 'Peter, I want to wash your feet. You don't understand now, but you will later.' I was so upset. I said, 'Jesus, you will never wash my feet!'

"Jesus then said something that pierced my heart: 'Peter, if you don't let me wash your feet, I cannot share my life with you.' I cried out, 'Jesus! Then wash not only my feet, but my hands and my head, as well.' Jesus looked up at me, poured water over my feet, and dried them with the towel. Next he did

> **Scripture Memory Verse**
>
> "If I, your Lord and Teacher, have washed your feet, you also ought to wash one another's feet."
>
> (John 13:14)

the same for John, then James, then the rest of us. When he had finished, he said, 'Now, as I have washed your feet, wash each other's feet.' A silence filled the whole room as we thought about what he meant by those words.

"After Jesus had put his outer robe back on, he sat down again at the table. I thought the celebration was almost over, but I was about to be surprised for a second time that evening. Jesus stood up. He took unleavened bread from the table, blessed it, and broke it. Jesus then looked around the table at us and said, 'Take and eat. This is my body.' I took a piece of the bread. Next Jesus took his cup and filled it with wine. He gave thanks to his heavenly Father. Looking at us, he said, 'This is my blood, which is poured out for many for the forgiveness of sins.' I took a sip from the cup and passed it on to James. I closed my eyes and repeated Jesus' words, 'This is my body. This is my blood.' I knew that this was a special moment."

Jesus, Speak to Me

At first it was difficult for Peter to accept that I came to serve and not to be served. But that truth changed his life. Later, because Peter wanted to follow in my footsteps, he too became a great servant. He was the first pope—the servant of servants!

There are many people who serve my Church. Priests serve the Church in a very special way. They repeat my words every time they say Mass in order to consecrate the bread and wine that become my body and blood. When a priest is ordained, he receives a special sacrament called Holy Orders. This sacrament gives the priest the grace to serve the people of God.

Everyone is called to serve me and the Church, but some people are called in a special way to become a priest or a religious brother or sister. These people decide not to marry and have children so that they can devote their whole lives to building my kingdom. What a gift they are to me! Perhaps someday I will call you to serve me in this way.

Prayer

Father, bless all those who serve you. Holy Spirit, touch our hearts so that we will answer your call to devote our lives to you.

The Garden of Gethsemane

(Mark 14:32–42; Luke 22:47–53)

Greetings from Samuel. Yesterday you heard about how Jesus washed the feet of his disciples and gave them his body to eat and his blood to drink. James, Jesus' disciple, told us that this is what happened next:

"I'll never forget Jesus' words during the Passover. I felt as though he was speaking just to me. He said, 'You must serve one another.' Jesus wanted us to help him on that Passover evening, but I didn't do a very good job. Let me tell you what happened.

"We stayed in the upper room talking and singing psalms together until it was really late. It seemed to me that Jesus just didn't want the Passover celebration to end. I didn't, either. At last he said, 'It is time to leave.' I wondered if we would go to Bethany to the home of Martha, Mary, and Lazarus. Jesus looked at all of us and said, 'I'm going to spend the night praying. Come with me.'

"I was walking next to Peter along the dark, narrow streets of the city. The moon was hidden behind the clouds. The only light was the occasional oil lamp burning in the window of a house. I was happy to spend the night with Jesus while he prayed. Jesus didn't say much as we walked along, except for one thing that really upset me: 'You will all leave me tonight.' Peter, who was often the first one of us to say or do something, exclaimed, 'Not me! I won't. Even if everyone else leaves you, I'll stay with you. If they put you to death, I'll die with you.' Oh, Peter was so sincere. He really meant what he said. But Jesus looked at him and said, 'Peter, not only will you run away, but before the cock crows tomorrow morning, you will have denied me three times.' Peter looked shocked and didn't say another word.

> **Remember**
>
> Jesus knows what it is like to suffer. Whenever you are suffering, you can always talk to him. No problem is too small to bring to Jesus.

"Once we were outside the city gate, Jesus led us across the Kidron Valley. We then started to climb a path up the Mount of Olives. I knew then where we were going. Jesus was taking us to the Garden of Gethsemane, one of his favorite places to pray. We had often been there with him. As we entered the garden, Jesus said, 'Stay here while I go over there and pray.' I was just about to sit down under an olive tree when Jesus said, 'Peter, James, and John, come with me.' We followed him. I watched Jesus go over to a large stone and kneel down. There wasn't a noise in the garden. The next sound I heard was Jesus saying, 'Couldn't you stay awake with me and pray?' I had fallen asleep! I was so embarrassed. I looked over to Peter and John, and they too had been asleep.

"Jesus left us again. This time I heard him praying in a loud voice, 'Father, please don't let me suffer. But if it is your will, I will do as you wish.' I don't know how long he prayed like that, because once again, I fell asleep. I opened my eyes when I heard Jesus say, 'Wake up! Could you not stay awake and pray just one hour with me?' I knew I had failed Jesus again. I looked at him and

Scripture Memory Verse

"Not my will but yours be done."

(Luke 22: 42)

saw sweat and drops of blood trickling down his face. I remembered that I had wanted to help others. But I couldn't even help Jesus by staying awake and praying with him. He was suffering terribly and needed my help.

"Again Jesus went off to pray. I am sorry to admit this, but a third time we all fell asleep. We woke up to the voice of someone shouting, 'Where is he?' I jumped up just as Jesus came toward us. 'My betrayer is here,' whispered Jesus.

"That's when I saw Judas and one of the Temple priests in the light of a soldier's torch. My heart sank. What was happening? Why were Roman soldiers here? Judas went up to Jesus. 'Master, it is good to find you here,' he said, and gave Jesus a kiss. That was the signal for the soldiers to grab Jesus.

"Peter—again the first to act—grabbed one of the soldiers' swords and cut off the ear of the priest's servant. But Jesus said, 'No violence.' Jesus put his hand on the side of the servant's head and healed him.

"I watched from behind a tree as the soldiers bound Jesus' arms together behind his back and pushed him toward the gate of the garden. I didn't know where they were taking him. I was too afraid to ask. I followed, but not so close that I would be seen."

Jesus, Speak to Me

The night that I spent in the Garden of Gethsemane was very, very hard for me. I knew that the next day I was going to be crucified. I had read the words of the prophet Isaiah, who foretold my death. I was scared. I knew that death on a cross would be extremely painful. I didn't want to suffer. So I asked my Father to change his mind. But I also loved and trusted my Father so much that I only wanted what he wanted. He knew what was best.

Sometimes you don't get your own way because my Father knows that his way will bring you closer to me. He sometimes allows difficult circumstances to bring about something better. God wants you to trust in him, even when you think something different should happen in your life. Can you think of an example when something good came out of something bad? Write it down in your journal so you don't forget how much my Father loves you, even in troubled times.

Prayer

Jesus, I pray that all those who are suffering may know that you have not forgotten them.

Peter's Denial

(Matthew 26:57–75; Mark 14:53–72)

Samuel, here again. Yesterday, you heard how Jesus took his disciples with him to the Garden of Gethsemane. While they were there, the disciples fell asleep, Judas betrayed Jesus, and Jesus was arrested. Today, Peter tells the story about how he denied Jesus:

"Jesus was arrested in the middle of the night. Because it was still dark, John and I were able to follow the soldiers without being seen. Although we were scared, we wanted to stay close to Jesus. The iron nails on the soles of the soldiers' sandals made a clinking sound on the stone streets as the soldiers commanded, 'Walk faster! The high priest is waiting for you.' I realized that we were walking toward the house of Caiaphas.

"As we got closer, I saw some scribes and elders of the Temple as well as members of the Sanhedrin—the powerful Jewish council—going in through the gate. I was shocked and worried. I had to find out what was going to happen to Jesus. I had so many questions running through my mind. 'Why would all these important people be gathering together in the middle of the night? Did they think Jesus was dangerous? What would they decide to do with Jesus?" I decided that I couldn't leave Jesus. Not now, not ever!

"Once John and I went through the gate into the courtyard, we separated. John disappeared into the crowd of soldiers and servants from the house. I walked around the sides of the courtyard. I didn't want to be seen or questioned about why I was there. It was a cold night, and some soldiers had lit a fire to keep themselves warm. Being tired made the night seem even colder, so I moved closer to the fire. That was a big mistake. One of the servant girls saw my face in the light. 'I've seen you before,' she said. 'You have traveled with the man inside—Jesus of Galilee.' I said the first thing that came to my mind: 'I don't know what you're talking about.'

> **Remember**
>
> Jesus wants me to always tell the truth, even if I'm afraid of being punished.

"Relieved that the servant girl didn't ask any more questions, I moved away from the fire and sat down under a window outside the place where Jesus was being a questioned. I heard the high priest ask, 'Does anyone know of anything wrong that this man has done?' Someone replied, 'This man says that he can destroy the Temple and rebuild it in three days.'

"There was more silence, and then a voice, which I assumed was that of Caiaphas, said, 'Why don't you answer? Is what they say true?' Jesus didn't reply. Then the same voice said, 'Tell us. Are you the Christ, the Son of God?' I heard Jesus answer, 'You have said it.' I was surprised to hear the sound of cloth ripping. It was the high priest tearing his robes. 'What blasphemy!' Caiaphas cried. 'He deserves death!'

"Suddenly another servant girl recognized me. She said to her friends, 'See that man over there? I've seen him with Jesus of Nazareth.' Again without thinking, I said, 'I swear I don't know that man.'

Scripture Memory Verse

"The truth will make you free."

(John 8:32)

"Afraid of any more questions, I got up and started walking toward the corner of the courtyard. But I didn't get far before someone shouted, 'Stop! I'm sure you are one of that man's disciples. You even talk like him. Yes! Your accent is from Galilee. That's where he is from. You must know him.' Now I was worried and angry. 'I've told you, I don't know the man,' I said.

"Just then the cock crowed. I remembered what Jesus had said: 'Peter, before the cock crows, you will deny knowing me three times.' I was devastated. I had boasted to Jesus that I would never do such a thing, but I had done it, just the same. Why did I say I didn't know him? Why couldn't I have said, 'Yes, of course I know him. I'm one of his closest friends!' Why was I such a coward? I ran out of the courtyard and into the street, sobbing, 'Jesus, I'm so sorry! Jesus, forgive me.'"

Jesus, Speak to Me

I know that Peter really loved me. He had left everything to follow me. But when it came to a big test, he failed. He lied about knowing me. It wasn't that he didn't love me, but he was afraid that if he told the truth about knowing me, he might be arrested or punished.

Are there times when you have lied because you were afraid of getting punished? The next time you are tempted to lie, ask the Holy Spirit to give you the courage to be honest. I love honesty. If you are always honest, your parents and your friends will always trust you. They will know that whatever you say is true. That will be a great witness of how much you love me.

Prayer

Jesus, please help me to always tell the truth.

After Peter received my Holy Spirit at Pentecost, he was never afraid again to tell people that he knew me. Peter suffered consequences for telling the truth—he was whipped and eventually crucified, just like me. But thousands of people believed him when he told them that I was their Savior!

A Family Journey with Jesus through Lent
Holy Week

Jesus' Sentencing, Whipping, and Crowning with Thorns

(Matthew 27:11–31)

This is John, one of Jesus' disciples. I'm going to continue the story where Peter left off. Every day I'll tell you about the events that led up to Jesus' death on the cross. Peter will finish the story by telling you some wonderful news. But first, let me tell you what happened when Jesus was brought before Pilate:

As the sun began to rise that Friday morning, I knew I had to find out what had happened to Jesus. I retraced my steps to Caiaphas' house. There I overheard some of the servants saying that the chief priests and soldiers had taken Jesus to Pilate, the Roman governor.

Judas, the disciple who betrayed Jesus, had also heard that the chief priests wanted to put Jesus to death. This really upset him. He immediately took the thirty pieces of silver back to the high priests, telling them, "I have betrayed an innocent man." They just laughed at him. When they wouldn't take back the money, Judas threw it at them. We later heard that Judas had died by hanging himself from a tree.

As I ran toward the Praetorium—the name for Pilate's house—I was surprised to see so many people in the courtyard. They were all waiting for Pilate to come out from the judgment hall. A man standing nearby told me, "The chief priests are accusing Jesus of making himself a king and telling the people not to pay taxes to Caesar. But Pilate doesn't think Jesus deserves to die."

> **Remember**
> God loves all his children and doesn't want us to hurt each other—with either our actions or our words.

When Pilate came out of the judgment hall, the crowd became very quiet. "I don't think this man has done anything wrong," he said. After a slight pause, Pilate continued, "Every year at Passover I release a criminal. Who shall I release this year? Do you want me to release Jesus, or this murderer, Barabbas?" I expected everyone to shout, "Jesus!" And some of us did. But more people started to shout, "Barabbas! Barabbas! Barabbas!" Their voices got louder and louder, and finally they drowned us out. "Enough!" said Pilate. "I will release Barabbas to you. But what shall I do with Jesus of Nazareth?" I couldn't believe my ears when the crowd shouted, "Crucify him! Crucify him!" "Very well," said Pilate. He seemed worried that he might cause a riot if he didn't hand Jesus over to be crucified. But he ordered a bowl of water to be brought to him, and he washed his hands before us. "I am innocent of this man's blood," he said.

Several soldiers led Jesus into the courtyard. I saw what they were doing to him, and it made me want to weep. They took off his clothing and tied him to a pole. Then they took turns striking Jesus with leather whips that had bits of bone tied to the ends. I counted the lashes—forty in all! Jesus was bleeding all over his shoulders, back, arms, and legs. What horrible pain—but he didn't cry out or complain.

Scripture Memory Verse

"Love is patient; love is kind."

(1 Corinthians 13:4)

Some soldiers were watching as Jesus was whipped. "How can we make him look like a king?" one asked. "He needs a royal robe!" said another. They found one and placed it over his bleeding shoulders. "He needs a crown," mocked another soldier. So he searched for branches with large thorns and twisted them into a crown. "Look what I have for you, Jesus," he said, as he pushed the crown of thorns into Jesus' head. All the soldiers started laughing at Jesus. Some got on their knees before him and said, "Hail, king of the Jews!" Others were spitting at him. I closed my eyes; I couldn't watch any longer. After what seemed like an eternity to me, the soldiers led Jesus away to be crucified.

Jesus, Speak to Me

Why do you think the soldiers wanted to mock me? Perhaps they were bored and wanted to have some fun. I was in great pain after the lashings I received. They hurt me by their actions, but when the soldiers made fun of me, I was also hurt by their words. It's so easy to hurt others by the words you say. Everyone is a child of God, created in his image and likeness. It upsets me when my Father's children insult or mock one another, say cruel things, or gossip. Please try to speak to everyone—and about everyone—with kindness.

Do you ever wonder why my Father allowed ordinary Roman soldiers to treat me, his only Son, the way they did? He wanted you to know how much he loves you. He loves you so much that he was willing to let me suffer whatever was necessary in order to save you. Don't ever forget that!

Prayer

Jesus, thank you for all the suffering that you went through on my behalf. Holy Spirit, help me to use my tongue to be kind to others.

Jesus Carries His Cross and Meets His Mother

(Matthew 27:55–56)

John continues his story:

After Jesus was arrested in the Garden of Gethsemane, I followed him to Caiaphas' house and then to Pilate's Praetorium. As soon as I realized what was going to happen to Jesus, I knew I had to tell his mother, Mary. On the way all I could think was, "How am I going to tell Jesus' mother that her son is going to be crucified?"

When I arrived, Mary was waiting at the door of the house where she was staying. "John," she asked, "have they arrested Jesus? Is he going to be crucified?" I told her everything I knew. She got up immediately and said, "John, I must go to Jesus. I want to be near my son on his way to his crucifixion."

> **Remember**
> Mary is Jesus' mother, my mother, and the Mother of the Church. I can ask her to pray for me at any time.

The midmorning air was hot and humid as we walked to the Praetorium. Just as we arrived, Jesus came out of the courtyard, covered in blood and struggling under the weight of a large wooden cross. "What have they done to him?" Mary gasped. I told her that Jesus had been whipped forty times by the Roman soldiers. Tears filled Mary's eyes. Together we followed as Jesus dragged the cross along the narrow stone streets toward the city gate. Whenever Jesus stopped for a moment, the soldiers tugged at the rope around his waist and ordered him to keep moving.

I knew that Jesus must be in terrible pain. His body was bloody from the lashings, the rough wood of the cross dug into his shoulder, and the crown of thorns pierced his head. We weren't the only ones following Jesus—a long procession had formed behind him. Crucifixions happened regularly here, and many people liked to watch the condemned make their way to the hill of execution, called Calvary.

Suddenly Jesus staggered and fell. Mary grabbed my arm in horror. She told me afterward that when she saw Jesus fall, it felt as if a sword had pierced her heart. Others around us laughed at him, saying, "Look, he's not even able to carry his own cross!" The soldiers had no pity for Jesus. Some kicked him, and others lashed him with their whips. I said to Mary, "I can't bear to see Jesus treated like this. He's not a criminal—he's an innocent man!" Mary looked up at me and said, "John, it has to be this way. Jesus must suffer and die for the sins of the world."

Jesus struggled to his feet, his knees bloodied from the fall. As he began to move forward, Mary let go of my arm and rushed over to him. "Jesus, I'm here," she said. He looked up for a moment into the eyes of his mother. A woman in the crowd shouted, "That's his mother. Let her talk to him." I will never forget that meeting between Jesus and Mary. All she wanted to do was to be near Jesus and to comfort him.

> **Scripture Memory Verse**
>
> "Blessed are you among women, and blessed is the fruit of your womb."
>
> (Luke 1:42)

My mind flashed back to the stories that Mary had told me. One day many years ago, an angel had appeared to her and said, "God wants you to have a baby. His name will be Jesus, and he will reign forever." Mary was confused because she wasn't even married yet, but she said yes to God. How I loved hearing her stories about Jesus' birth—with the angels praising God, and the shepherds and wise men coming to adore and worship her infant son.

My daydreaming was shattered by the soldiers' orders. "Stop talking," they said to Mary. "That's long enough. Get back." I stepped forward and took Mary by the arm. Together we moved back into the crowd. Some women came and comforted Mary in her grief. My heart, too, was breaking as I watched Jesus walk to his death.

Jesus, Speak to Me

My mother, Mary, knew that I would take upon myself the punishment for the sins of the whole world. It was so hard for her to watch me struggling to carry the cross to Calvary. I love my mother very much. I was so sorry that she had to see me suffer. I'm grateful that John was with her that day to support and comfort her. After I died, John took her into his home. It was a great comfort to me to see my mother nearby as I carried the cross, and to know that she was praying for me.

Did you know that Mary is not only my mother but your mother as well? Our Father chose her from the beginning of time to be my mother and to be the Mother of the Church. That means that she loves you and cares about you, just like any mother would love and care for her child. You can pray to her at any time, and she will come to me on your behalf. She will comfort you as she comforted me. That's one reason why one of my mother's titles is "Help of Christians."

Prayer

Jesus, thank you so much for Mary, my mother. Holy Spirit, please bless my own mother with your gifts of peace and joy.

Simon of Cyrene Helps Jesus Carry His Cross

(Luke 23:26–31)

John continues:

After his short meeting with his mother, Jesus took a deep breath and once again started dragging the cross behind him. Mary and I stayed as close to Jesus as we could, without getting in the way of the soldiers. As we passed through the gate leading out of the city, I saw the rocky hill of Calvary ahead. I said to Mary, "How is Jesus going to carry his cross over those rocks and manage to climb up there?" Mary replied, "I don't know, John. But I do know that his Father will help him."

I was very worried about Jesus. He was already showing signs of exhaustion—staggering from side to side and gasping for breath. He hadn't slept all night. He was in severe pain, and he had lost a great deal of blood from the forty lashes at the pillar. I couldn't take my eyes off him. But it was so hard to watch the Roman soldiers mistreat him. They had no pity for Jesus as they tugged harder on the rope around his waist and kicked and whipped him. All they seemed to want was to get to Calvary as quickly as possible. To them, Jesus was just another criminal. They knew they wouldn't get their day's pay until he was dead.

> **Remember**
> You never have to carry a cross alone. Your heavenly Father will always give you someone to help you.

I was afraid that every step Jesus took would be his last. Then I overhead one of the soldiers say, "We need to find someone to help this man. If not, he's going to collapse before we get him crucified." Usually criminals had to carry their own crosses. One of the soldiers shouted to a bystander, "You, over there. Come here!" He grabbed the man and asked him, "What's your name?" The man replied, "I'm Simon from Cyrene, a farmer visiting from the country." One of the soldiers laughed. "Good—a farmer. You should be strong enough. Help this man carry his cross up that hill." I don't know what went through Simon's mind, but he went over and picked up Jesus' cross. Jesus would not have to carry his cross alone.

With Simon's help, Jesus continued his agonizing walk up the rocky hill. The heavy wooden beams, balanced on his sore and bleeding shoulder, made it difficult for him to look up. Suddenly he fell to the ground again, this time with his face in the dirt. Mary cried out, "Jesus!" A soldier barked, "Simon, get him up." Simon put his arm around Jesus' waist and helped him to regain his balance under the cross.

Some women who knew Jesus were standing along the side of the road. They had been singing and waving palms as he entered Jerusalem. But today they were weeping and wailing. Jesus stopped. His throat was dry. In a rasping whisper he said, "Daughters of Jerusalem, do not weep for me, but weep for yourselves and for your children." With only a few hours to live, Jesus' message was still the same: Repent! Jesus was inviting them to cry over the ways that they and their children had disobeyed his Father.

> ## Scripture Memory Verse
>
> "If any want to become my followers, let them deny themselves and take up their cross and follow me."
>
> (Matthew 16:24)

It was very hot that Friday, and Jesus hadn't had anything to drink since the night before. The soldiers seemed to be getting more and more impatient with him. I watched as he stumbled over the rocky path leading to the top of Calvary. A few more yards, I thought, and the walk will be over. But Jesus had no strength left. I saw him fall again.

Jesus, Speak to Me

When I had so much trouble carrying my cross alone, my Father sent Simon of Cyrene to help me. I didn't have to bear the burden by myself.

Is there someone you know who is carrying a cross? Ask my Holy Spirit to make you aware of the crosses that some people have to bear. Maybe you have a friend who is struggling with an illness, who is having difficulty at school, or whose parents are out of work. Perhaps you could send a card, visit, or make a phone call. My Spirit will give you ideas of how to help. Most importantly, let that person know how much you care.

When I see people helping each other to carry their crosses, it shows me how much they love each other and are willing to sacrifice for one another.

Prayer

Father, thank you that you give me opportunities to help bear the burdens of others.

Jesus Is Stripped and Nailed to the Cross

(Mark 15:22–32)

John continues:

Once Jesus reached the top of Calvary, the soldiers took the cross from him. Simon of Cyrene disappeared into the crowd. I often wonder if Jesus said anything to Simon before he left. As Mary and I stood on the hill, we heard the cries of two criminals who were being nailed to their crosses. The whole crowd became very quiet. A soldier gave Jesus a mug of cheap wine, but he refused to drink it.

"Come on! Let's get this one ready for crucifixion," one of the soldiers called out. Mary squeezed my arm as we watched the soldiers roughly rip off Jesus' cloak. One, two, three tugs were needed where parts of his tunic were stuck to his body with dried blood. Jesus was now naked except for a loincloth.

> **Remember**
>
> All your sins have been forgiven by my sacrifice on the cross.

I looked over at Jesus and gasped. He was about to fall again. But the soldiers grabbed him and led him to his cross, which was lying on the ground. They pushed him down backwards onto the cross. His bruised body hit the wood hard; the crown of thorns bounced off the ground. Four soldiers stretched out his arms and legs to match them up with the holes in the wood. A large wooden nail was hammered into each of his hands, and one through both of his feet. Then the four soldiers lifted the heavy cross on which hung Jesus, the Savior of the world. It swayed to and fro as it was dropped into a deep hole. I heard Jesus say, "Father, forgive them; they don't know what they are doing."

Off to one side, I heard the soldiers arguing. "I want this one." "No! You got them from the last criminal." "I think we should divide them all equally." They were arguing about Jesus' clothes. They couldn't decide who would get his garments. So the tunic they tore into pieces, and each of them got the same-sized piece. But because his cloak was made from a single piece of woven material—without any seams—they decided to roll dice to see which of them would get it. The winner got the whole cloak.

There was still quite a crowd of people watching the crucifixion. Their words were directed at Jesus. They mocked and jeered him. If he was able to perform so many wondrous miracles, why didn't he just get off the cross? "Aha," some of them said. "You who would destroy the Temple and rebuild it in three days, save yourself and come down from the cross!" Others said, "Let the Messiah, the king of Israel, come down from the cross so that we may see and believe." I hoped that Jesus couldn't hear these words, yet I was sure that he had.

Pilate had an inscription written and ordered it to be placed on the cross over Jesus' head. It read, "Jesus of Nazareth, the King of the Jews." The Jewish leaders didn't like it. I heard one of them complain that the plaque should have said, "This man claimed to be the King of the Jews." But Pilate wouldn't listen to them, and said, "What I have written, I have written."

> **Scripture Memory Verse**
>
> "And forgive us our sins, for we ourselves forgive everyone indebted to us."
>
> (Luke 11:4)

Jesus was between the crosses of the two criminals also crucified that day. One of the criminals said to Jesus, "Aren't you the Messiah? Then save yourself and us!" "Don't say that!" rebuked the other criminal. "We have done wrong. We deserve to die. But this man has done nothing wrong." Turning to Jesus, he said, "Jesus, remember me when you come into your kingdom." Jesus was so pleased with this condemned man's faith that he said to him, "I want you to know that today you will be with me in paradise!"

Jesus, Speak to Me

As the nails were being hammered into my hands and feet, I was thinking about you. I knew that I was the only one who could pay the penalty for your sins. I wasn't blaming you for my suffering. My heart was full of forgiveness for all of your sins.

I willingly took your sins upon myself and became the perfect, unblemished sacrificial Lamb—just as in Old Testament times. I redeemed you. The price you owed God for disobeying him was paid by me. Yes, all of your sins were washed away with my blood, even those that you might think are too big for me to forgive. So rejoice in my great love for you!

Today I especially ask you to forgive anyone who has hurt you in any way. Please don't hold any grudges. Remember that I have forgiven all your sins. So forgive as you have been forgiven. Look into your heart now to see if there is anyone that you need to forgive. Watch out for thoughts such as, "They hurt me. They don't deserve my forgiveness."

Talk with one another about forgiving and not holding grudges. Pray for anyone in your family who is having a hard time forgiving.

> **Prayer**
>
> Jesus, thank you for forgiving my sins. Holy Spirit, help me to forgive everyone who has ever hurt me.

Jesus' Death and Burial

(Matthew 27:45–66; John 19:25–42)

John speaking:

As Jesus hung on the cross from the sixth hour to the ninth hour—noon to three o'clock—the sky got so dark that it looked like night. Mary and I were now right under Jesus' cross. Jesus knew that we were there. He looked down at his mother and said, "Woman, this is your son." Jesus meant me. Then Jesus looked at me and said, "Behold your mother." Jesus was telling Mary and me to take care of each other. He was also telling the world that Mary was the mother of us all.

For three hours Jesus hung on the cross. I kept thinking, "Jesus, you are dying for my sins and for the sins of all the people who have been or will ever be born." Jesus was in such terrible pain. He must have felt very alone, although Mary and I were there with him. I also saw Mary Magdalene and Mary, the mother of James, very near to us. Suddenly Jesus cried out, "My God, my God, why have you forsaken me?"

Just moments before Jesus died, he said, "I thirst." One of the soldiers soaked a sponge in vinegar, placed it on a long reed, and held it up to Jesus' mouth. The last words that Jesus said were, "It is finished." I turned to Mary and said, "Jesus has died."

> **Remember**
>
> When Jesus died on the cross, the power of sin and Satan was destroyed.

The moment Jesus died, the earth began to shake under our feet. When a centurion who was in charge that day felt the earthquake, he said, "Truly this man was God's Son!" Later I heard that the curtain in the Temple separating the holiest place from the place where people prayed had been torn in two, from top to bottom.

The criminals on either side of Jesus were still alive. The soldiers broke their legs so that they would die more quickly. Jesus was obviously dead, so they didn't bother to break his legs. But I watched as a soldier took his sword and pierced Jesus' side. Blood and water poured out.

Because it was the eve of the Sabbath, the bodies had to be taken down before sunset. It was against the Jewish law for the bodies to remain on the cross after that time. Joseph, a rich man from Arimathea who was also a Pharisee and a secret follower of Jesus, approached Mary. "Mary, I have received permission from Pilate to take Jesus' body down from the cross. In a nearby garden, I have a new tomb cut out of rock, in which we can bury him." "Thank you, Joseph," said Mary.

A ladder was placed against Jesus' cross. The nails were gently removed from Jesus' hands and feet. With sheets Jesus was slowly lowered to the ground. His body was placed into Mary's open arms. I will always remember Mary holding

Scripture Memory Verse

"For God so loved the world that he gave his only Son, so that everyone who believes in him may not perish but may have eternal life."

(John 3:16)

Jesus so lovingly for the last time. Perhaps she was thinking back to the first time she had held him in the stable in Bethlehem.

Jesus' body was carried to the new tomb. It was such a sad procession. Nicodemus, another Pharisee and follower of Jesus, was with us. When we got to the garden tomb, Joseph and Nicodemus anointed Jesus' body with oils made from a mixture of myrrh and aloes. Jesus' body was then wrapped in white linen burial cloths. Inside the tomb, his body was laid on one of the rocky ledges that had been cut into the wall.

The sun was setting as the round stone was rolled over the entrance to the tomb. I heard Mary Magdalene and some of the other women say that they planned to come back on the first day of the week to anoint Jesus' body with more oils. Sadly we all walked away from the tomb, crying and comforting one another.

Even though Jesus was dead, the Pharisees were still worried. They went to Pilate and asked for soldiers to be sent to the tomb to guard it. They also asked that a seal be put on the stone that we had rolled against the entrance. Why? The Pharisees had heard Jesus say, "After three days I will rise again." They didn't believe Jesus, but they thought that we disciples would sneak back to the tomb, take Jesus' body, and bury it somewhere else. Then we would tell everyone that Jesus had risen from the dead, just like he said he would. So Pilate ordered some soldiers to guard the tomb, as the Pharisees had requested.

But all of us were in for a big surprise!

Jesus, Speak to Me

The last words that I said from the cross were, "It is finished!" That was my cry of triumph. The work that my Father had sent me to do was completed. That is why you can call the day that I suffered and died *Good Friday.*

What was finished? Let me explain! First, when I died on the cross, the power of sin was destroyed. The gates of heaven—which had been closed since the sin of Adam and Eve—were opened again. Second, through my death on the cross, Satan was defeated. By the power of my Holy Spirit living in you, you can now say no to all of Satan's temptations.

As I hung on the cross I thought of my Father's great love for you. Do you know how much he loves you? Listen carefully! If you had been the only person in the world, my Father would still have sent me into the world to die for your sins. He wants you to spend eternity with him!

Spend a little time today kneeling before a crucifix. I want to speak to your heart in a special way. And don't forget to recall my last words, because they are words of victory: "It is finished!"

Prayer

Jesus, I thank you with all my heart for dying on the cross for my sins. I love you, and I want to live with you forever in heaven!

holy week | day 6

The Resurrection

(John 20:1–29)

This is Peter, and I want to tell you the amazing end of the story! Jesus was full of surprises! I've told you that before. Now I want to tell you about the most wonderful surprise I've ever had in my whole life!

After Jesus died on the cross, all of his disciples gathered together again. We talked and cried for hours and hours—not only about our last days with Jesus and his death on the cross, but also about everything that had happened since he called us to follow him. I told everyone how I had denied knowing Jesus. But I also knew that Jesus had forgiven me. We felt so terribly sad and alone. We had loved being with Jesus, but now he was dead. We were afraid of what would happen to us. There were many, many people here in Jerusalem who knew that we were followers of Jesus. So we didn't even go outside. We kept the doors of the house locked.

It was the third day after Jesus had died—the first day of the week—and John and I had woken up before everyone else. I said, "John, what are we going to do? We can't stay locked up in this house forever." Suddenly, there was loud banging on the door. Then I heard, "Open up! Let me in. It's Mary Magdalene." I opened the door very slowly and let her in. She told us the most amazing story.

She had gone very early with Salome and with James' mother, Joanna, to the garden tomb. Just as they had planned, they brought along some very special oils to anoint Jesus' body. But when they got to the tomb, they found that the stone had been rolled away and that the soldiers Pilate had sent to guard the tomb were asleep. The women were crying and comforting one another when two angels appeared to them and said, "Do not be afraid. You are looking for Jesus of Nazareth. He has risen, just as he said he would. He is not here. See the place where he was laid. Why do you look for the living among the dead? Go and tell his disciples."

> **Remember**
>
> What do you want to remember about Jesus? You decide. Write it down in your journal!

Mary Magdalene paused, and I said, "Mary, I don't believe you!" "Then come with me to the tomb!" she replied, challenging me. John and I quickly put on our sandals. We ran through the streets. It was still early, and there weren't many people around. We went out through the gate of the city and headed toward the tomb. I was out of breath and had to stop. John, who is much younger than I, kept running and reached the tomb first. He looked in, but didn't enter. When I arrived, I went in. I found the burial cloths neatly folded and lying on the ledge. I saw and I believed!

All the way back to the house, I kept saying to myself, "Jesus has risen from the dead!" What astounding news! But then I remembered how he had talked about being put to death and rising again. That evening, we saw Jesus with our own eyes. He came through our locked doors and stood among us! "Peace be with you," he said, and then showed us the wounds in his hands and his side. We were so excited to see Jesus! He was alive! We rejoiced. Jesus had defeated death!

> ### Scripture Memory Verse
>
> "The Lord has risen indeed."
>
> (Luke 24:34)

Now Thomas, one of the twelve disciples, wasn't with us when Jesus appeared the first time. We told him everything when he returned. But he didn't think we were telling the truth. "I won't believe unless I put my fingers where the nails were and put my hand in his side," Thomas said.

A week later, Jesus came again and stood in front of us, saying, "Peace be with you!" Then he turned to Thomas and said, "Put your fingers in my nail wounds and your hand in my side. Do not doubt, but believe!" Thomas exclaimed, "My Lord and my God!" "Oh Thomas," Jesus said, "blessed are the people who have not seen me, but still believe."

For forty days Jesus appeared to us at different times and in different places. It was always a great surprise! I knew that Jesus had forgiven me for denying him, because he asked me to feed his sheep. Jesus was trusting me to "feed" everyone with the truths of his great love!

Jesus told us to stay in Jerusalem until the Holy Spirit came upon us. It happened on the day of Pentecost. Now that I'm filled with the Holy Spirit, I'm no longer afraid of what might happen to me. I want to go and tell everyone that Jesus Christ has died for our sins, that we are forgiven, and that we can be filled with his Holy Spirit and live a new life. I'm even ready to die for Jesus!

Jesus, Speak to Me

This is such a day for rejoicing! I am alive! I have risen from the dead. I am Lord over sin, Satan, and death. I have won the victory! I will live forever.

Now I can be everywhere at the same time! I will never leave you. Whenever you think about me, know that I am there with you!

Prayer

Alleluia! Alleluia! He is risen!

Thank you for making me part of your life in a special way during these last forty days. Now that Lent is over, please keep me in the center of your life. Share with me what makes you happy, sad, afraid, or angry. Tell me anything. Trust me. Sit in my presence and soak up my love at home and at church. Shout out my praises. Boast about being a child of your heavenly Father. Call on my Holy Spirit for power to be holy. Enjoy being my friend. Share the good news of salvation with others. Look forward to heaven. And always remember that I love you!

A Family Journey with Jesus through Lent
Suggested Lenten Activities

Lent is a season rich in symbols and meaning. Here are some suggested ways to help you and your family grow spiritually during Lent. Choose the ones you think your family would enjoy the most.

Ash Wednesday
Attend Ash Wednesday services at your parish, and talk about the meaning of the ashes.

Family Fasts
Together as a family, decide on one or two things to fast from during Lent. Perhaps your family could give up eating at fast food restaurants or watching television on a designated evening of the week. Encourage one another along the way.

Lenten Candles
If your family enjoys Advent wreaths, set up seven candles in the shape of a cross to mark the weeks of Lent. Use purple candles for each week of Lent, but put a white one in the center or at the top for Easter Sunday.

Soup Suppers
Prepare a simple soup one night a week and deposit the money that you would have spent on dinner in the poor box at your church, or donate it to a charity. You may want to join other families in this practice or check out local parishes to see if they offer Lenten soup suppers.

A Saturday of Service
Select a Saturday in Lent and keep it free of other commitments. Spend the day with your family working on a service project. You might collect cans of food for the local food bank, serve at a soup kitchen, or visit a nursing home.

Pretzel Making

In the days of the very strict Lenten fasts, pretzels made from bread, water, and yeast were a staple food. They were shaped in the form of a person's arms crossed in prayer. Make homemade pretzels. Your kids will love rolling out the dough into pretzels—and eating them.

Stations of the Cross

For younger children, draw your own stations on construction paper. Place them around the house. One evening after dinner, visit each station with your children. Try to attend the Stations of the Cross at your parish several times during Lent.

Make a Pilgrimage

Is there a nearby shrine, monastery, or cathedral that you could visit? As part of your trip, explore the local history and pray together as a family. Stop for lunch afterward.

Pray the Sorrowful Mysteries of the Rosary

This is one of the most significant ways of reflecting on Jesus' suffering and death. To enhance the meaning of those events, find a scriptural rosary booklet in your local Catholic bookstore and read the verses relating to that mystery before each Hail Mary.

Be a "Secret Simon" of Cyrene

Put the names of all the members of your family into a bag. Each week during Lent, have everyone draw a name and keep it a secret. Every day that week, try to do something kind for that person, without letting him or her know who did it. One day you might write a note of encouragement before a test, or another day secretly perform a household chore. Try to keep one another's secrets for the week, even if you catch on. Then, at the end of the week, you can each try to guess who your "secret Simon" was.

Crosses for Christ:

On Ash Wednesday, make a big cross out of poster board and hang it in your kitchen or family room. Then cut out several dozen smaller crosses from construction paper and keep them nearby. Whenever a family member does something special for Jesus, he or she can tape a small cross to the big one. See how many little crosses your family joins with Jesus' cross during Lent!

Puppet Show

Choose a favorite gospel story from this book and put on a puppet show. Make simple puppets out of paper lunch bags or draw pictures and staple them to ice pop sticks. Have the children hide behind your sofa and act out the story with their puppets.

Activities for Holy Week

Make the Easter Triduum—Holy Thursday through Saturday—a special family time. These are holy days in the original sense of the word—days set apart to pray and fast in anticipation of the glory of Easter morning. Plan to go as a family, if possible, to the Holy Thursday and Good Friday services at your parish.

Christian Seder Meal

Join together with another family to celebrate a traditional seder meal. Such a meal usually includes roasted lamb, unleavened bread, and bitter herbs. Suggestions for menus and prayers can be found online.

Experience the Passion as a Family

On Good Friday, read the gospel account of Jesus' passion as a family. Assign parts to members of the family who are old enough to participate. Or, rent and watch a movie depicting the life and death of Jesus.

Holy Saturday Food Preparations:

It's the day to prepare traditional Easter foods, such as hot cross buns, Easter lamb cake, or an ethnic specialty, such as the English simnel cake. Mold butter into the shape of a lamb for breakfast Easter morning. If you're at a loss for recipes, search online. And don't forget to color the eggs and fill the Easter baskets.

Easter Vigil Mass:

If children are old enough, attend the Easter Vigil, which celebrates both the resurrection of our Lord and the initiation of members into the Church. If your children are too young, wake them early on Easter morning and watch the sunrise together outdoors as you sip hot chocolate and eat hot cross buns. Discuss the significance of the "Son-rise"—the rising of the Son of God!

Appendix

Themes for Each Day

Week 1

Day 1   Sacrament of Baptism
Day 2   Overcoming Satan's Temptations
Day 3   Giving Our Lives to Jesus
Day 4   Listening to the Holy Spirit

Week 2

Day 1   Spiritual Sight and Not Taking Things for Granted
Day 2   Examining Our Conscience and Making Things Right
Day 3   Staying Close to Jesus
Day 4   Interceding for Sick and Needy Children
Day 5   Overcoming Our Fears
Day 6   Memorizing Scripture

Week 3

Day 1   Generosity
Day 2   Gratitude
Day 3   God's Glory and Heaven
Day 4   Sharing the Good News
Day 5   Praying Every Day
Day 6   Sacrament of Reconciliation

Week 4

Day 1   Sacrament of the Anointing of the Sick
Day 2   God's Mercy
Day 3   The Eucharist
Day 4   The Treasure of Knowing Jesus
Day 5   Trusting
Day 6   Judging Others

Week 5

Day 1   Good and Bad Choices
Day 2   New Life in Christ
Day 3   Faith
Day 4   Helping Others
Day 5   Friendship
Day 6   Holy Mass, the Heavenly Banquet

Week 6

Day 1   Praising God
Day 2   Temples of the Holy Spirit
Day 3   Worshipping Idols
Day 4   Servants of the Church and Vocations
Day 5   Doing Our Father's Will
Day 6   Telling the Truth

Week 7

Day 1   Speaking Kindly
Day 2   Mary, Mother of Jesus
Day 3   Carrying Each Other's Crosses
Day 4   Forgiving Others
Day 5   Jesus' Mission Completed
Day 6   Jesus Is Risen!